A Never-Ending Battle

A Soldier's Ongoing Struggle with Combat PTSD

"It is a must read for the young veterans of Afghanistan and Iraq."

MSG Gregory H. Murry, U.S. Army (Ret)
Author of "Content With My Wages, A Sergeant's Story: Book I-Vietnam"

"Every mental health professional who has ever treated (or could ever have) a veteran as a client, also should read this book."

James P. Coan - Author of "Con Thien: The Hill of Angels"

"The book is a painfully honest reconstruction of his struggle that he wrote down in hopes of guiding other sufferers."

Michael Putzel - Author of "The Price They Paid: Enduring Wounds of War"

"Read this book and be changed forever."

"It gave me more insight to the workings of the VA."

"It was very eye-opening and enlightening."

"A must read for anyone...military or not."

"This book needs to be read, not just by veterans with PTSD and their families but also by current military personnel and anyone contemplating military service."

"This book should be required reading for war veterans."

"Strongly endorse and encourage all veterans to read this book."

"Howard courageously shares his story with the intent to spread awareness about the danger and darkness that can come after serving."

"It is rare that someone can take a frightening experience and present it accurately without falling victim to the emotions it will evoke."

A Never-Ending Battle

A Soldier's Ongoing Struggle with Combat PTSD

by

Sgt. Howard B. Patrick
Light Weapons Infantryman

To Del & Marcia

[signature]

AUTHOR'S NOTE

I have done my best to describe my Vietnam experiences as candidly and accurately as possible. I have read through my unit's mission reports at the National Archives, and have had numerous discussions with members of my unit about our experiences, yet there are probably some minor inaccuracies in what I have written because they are a reflection of how I remember the events, and the thoughts and feelings I had as those events unfolded. The characters in the book are all real, although fictitious names were used in some instances.

Copyright © 2015 by Howard B. Patrick

First Edition: January 2015

ISBN 10: 1507762909   ISBN 13: 978-1507762905

DEDICATION

This book is dedicated to my all fellow warriors who gave a part of themselves in service to their country and are still reliving the traumatic events of their wars. I hope what I've written provides a source of comfort to them in knowing they are not alone, and a source of guidance for them and their families to get started on a road to achieve some degree of tranquility in their lives.

Table of Contents

Prologue

For three straight days and nights Typhoon Bess unmercifully battered the hell out of my platoon with torrential rains and raging winds gusting in excess of 100 miles an hour. It was one of the worst storms to strike South Vietnam in many years, and to make matters worse random enemy small arms fire kept us stuck in our foxholes. Earlier, we had made contact with a small NVA patrol but the fast approaching storm caused both sides to dig in and wait it out. Our ammunition was dangerously low and what little food we took with us when we left our base camp was practically gone. The typhoon kept all aircraft grounded, preventing our helicopters from picking us up or even getting supplies to us. Our visibility was practically non-existent, and the howling winds made it impossible to hear any other sounds. The ferocious weather conditions also affected the NVA soldiers and lessened their ability to assault our positions, but it was possible they could try using it as cover to sneak close enough to toss grenades at us. We pissed in our pants when we had to urinate and cautiously crawled out of our holes to take a crap, hoping the trees we crept to would provide enough cover to keep our bare asses from getting hit by stray bullets. We were in two-man foxholes, and though we alternated standing watch, trying to sleep standing up in a hole filled chest-high with muddy water was just about impossible.

For me, those three days were some of the most nerve-racking I experienced during my entire time in Vietnam, even more than being in a firefight. When on a recon patrol or waiting to spring an ambush I always experienced some degree of anxiety, normally just the right amount to keep me focused and alert. The instant enemy contact was made and bullets started flying adrenaline would kick in, all thoughts got put on hold, and my training and experience instinctively took over. I reacted without having to think about what I needed to do, I just did it. But after a few hours in our water-filled hole, my foxhole comrade and I were all talked out, leaving us alone with our silent thoughts, prayers, and fears. My anxiety level was off the scale, yet if I hoped to stay alive, I had to keep vigilant and ready to act in spite of the pain, the stress, and the fear. I did my best to stay alert, but no matter how hard I tried it was practically impossible to prevent the same nagging questions from interrupting all other thoughts: Will I ever see my family again? Will I get out of here alive or is this it? Will this lousy hole in the ground become my grave?

I had been married for just over two years, and only a few short months earlier became the father of a beautiful baby girl. Never could I have imagined I would wind up in a war, yet there I was, in the middle of the most divisive war of the 20th century. In no way could I have ever thought I would be so easily transformed from a laid back, easy-going computer technician who placed a high value on life, into a combat hardened soldier, ready to kill without hesitation and without even the slightest bit of remorse. But that's exactly what I had become. When I ask myself how this could have happened, I'm sure my answer would match that of thousands of other soldiers who served in Vietnam— I was unlucky enough to get drafted. But put that same question to my wife and her answer would be quite different. To Judy, luck had nothing to do with it—it was fate, it was my destiny, it was meant to be. Although I was never much of a fatalist before Vietnam, a number of events that I experienced there—events in which I firmly believe I should have died—have led me to accept the fact there really must be something to it.

Chapter 1 – The Trigger

It was almost midnight on an unusually cool mid-summer night in Philadelphia. Judy and I were lying in bed, Nightline was still on, but we were dozing more than watching. I was mentally flipping a coin to decide whether I should get out of bed and turn the TV off, or leave it on 'til I got up the next morning. Just as I pictured the coin flying into the air the phone rang. I was used to middle-of-the-night calls from my days as a computer technician when I had to respond to off-hour emergencies, but for some reason that particular ring gave me a very uneasy feeling. It seemed to have a slightly different sound than normal, almost as if it was trying to convey a sense of urgency. Our two teenagers were already in bed, so that wasn't a concern, yet my stomach was already in knots as I reached for the phone. "Hopefully, it's just a wrong number," I said to myself as I put the receiver to my ear.

I nervously said hello, and a male voice asked "is this Howard Patrick?" Still a bit apprehensive, I said yes, and he followed that up with "were you in Vietnam with the First Cavalry Division in '69?" When I said yes again, he excitedly said "Howard, this is Chad, Chad Spawr. Sorry for the late call. My flight just landed and I'm in Philly on business, but only for a few days. I was hoping we could get together while I'm here." I was completely caught off guard and didn't quite know how to respond. I couldn't remember ever meeting anyone by the name of Chad in Vietnam or anywhere else, so I finally said "I'm sorry, but I don't remember you." After a brief silence he said "what about the guys we worked with in Civil Affairs—Lieutenant Mellitin, Scotty, Sammy or McGaha—do you remember any of them?" I drew a blank on those names as well. With disappointment in his voice, he mentioned some of the Civil Affairs and Psyops missions he said we were on together, and when I said none of that was familiar either there seemed to be nothing more to talk about. We hung up without making plans to meet, and I never even thought to ask him anything about himself, or even get his phone number. The call left me dazed and puzzled. It surprised, disturbed, and troubled me, all at the same time.

Judy only heard my end of the conversation, but she could tell the call had me pretty worked up. I filled her in, assured her I was okay, even though that was hardly the case, and spent the rest of the night not only wondering why I couldn't remember Chad or the other names he mentioned, but why I had so little recollection of my entire time in Vietnam. I knew I was a squad leader in a Recon Company and was later transferred to a Civil Affairs unit, but beyond that everything was very hazy. I couldn't even remember the last time I had thoughts about any of my army service.

During the next few weeks, I spent most nights lying in bed trying to remember anything else about Vietnam, with little success. I remembered my first year in the army—getting drafted, going through basic and advanced infantry training, even NCO school, where I trained to be a combat squad leader and graduated with the rank of sergeant. I remember getting to Vietnam in mid-June, being assigned to a recon company with the First Cavalry Division, and later being transferred to a Civil Affairs unit, but not much more. I was an infantryman in the middle of a jungle war, a squad leader in a recon platoon, and I came home with a Combat Infantry Badge, two Air Medals, and a Bronze Star. That told me unquestionably I had been in combat, but nothing more. What kind of combat situations was I in? They must have been pretty bad if I had completely blanked them out. What about the guys in my squad, in my platoon—who were they and did any of them get wounded or die? I had lots of questions but no answers. My frustration led to obsession. I couldn't think of any other time in my life that my mind was such a complete blank and it was driving me crazy.

Finally, after months of racking my brain day and night, I had a breakthrough—a dream about Vietnam. I was in jungle fatigues, flying over dense foliage in an army helicopter. There was a South Vietnamese soldier sitting on the rear seat, broadcasting in Vietnamese through a large speaker system that was hanging out of one of the open side doors. I was squatting on the floor in front of the other open door, tossing out propaganda leaflets. The messages were directed at the Viet Cong, telling them to give up their fight to overthrow the South Vietnam government. The loud noise of the engine and rotor blades muffled the sound of gunfire from below, but as soon as the chopper's two door gunners began firing their machine guns I knew VC on the ground were shooting at us. Getting shot at was a fairly regular occurrence on that type of mission, so I wasn't too concerned at first. But when red lights on the cockpit instrument panel started flashing, and the normal chopper sounds were suddenly much quieter, I knew we were in deep shit. Warning bells suddenly sounded and I was sure we were going to crash. Everything was happening in slow motion—seconds seemed to be taking minutes. The pilot was struggling with the control lever between his legs, the copilot was flipping switches, and the helicopter was making a jerky turn as it began losing altitude. The door gunners were still firing their M-60s, which have a firing rate of 500-600 rounds per minute, yet the empty shell casings were ejecting slowly enough for me to count them. The Vietnamese soldier's lips were moving but there were no sounds coming from them. I think he was praying. I was scared shitless.

Suddenly I was sitting up in my bed, drenched in sweat and trembling all over. My stomach was in knots and my heart felt as though it was going to beat its way out of my chest. I didn't remember ever feeling as scared as I was at that moment. Judy was still asleep, so I left the bedroom and walked around the house until I calmed down enough to think about what just happened. As my mind cleared, I realized that I remembered every detail of the dream, which was something that rarely happened to me. I wasn't certain I had been reliving an actual event, but it was so real I felt it must have been something I lived through. And, in a strange way, I felt pleased with myself—pleased that my determination enabled me to overcome a barrier that was affecting me so much. My family life, my job performance, even my health had been suffering from my obsession to remember Vietnam. But at that moment I felt confident

19

the dream would lead to my buried memories surfacing, which I believed would enable me to get my life back to normal. Never did I think it would result in just the opposite.

Over the next few months that same dream became a fairly regular occurrence. It always started and ended exactly the same, always in slow motion, and I always woke up scared, shaking, and soaking wet. I still wasn't able to remember Chad, the names of other guys I served with, or anything else about my time in Vietnam, but I was convinced the dream was a replay of an actual event that I had experienced. Nevertheless, I didn't know what to do. I knew the memories were locked up somewhere inside my head, but didn't know how to get them unlocked. And I wasn't even sure that I should. A part of me thought I might be better off to just forget the whole thing. Forget Chad's call, and let the Vietnam memories stay hidden from me. I buried them for a reason, and digging them up after all these years might turn out to be harmful. But it was too late for that. I knew I wouldn't be able to stop wondering about them. It would eat away at me until I remembered, so I had to find a way to make that happen. Maybe if I thought back through my first year in the army—from being drafted to arriving in Vietnam—maybe that would jog those memories back into my consciousness. Nothing else was working, so I thought it was worth a try.

Chapter 2 – The Beginning

As required, I registered for the draft when I turned 18, but since we were not involved in any military conflicts at the time I never gave much thought to the possibility of actually getting drafted. I spent the next three years in college, first as a full-time student, followed by two years part-time at night. When I realized college wasn't working for me I entered a two-year Electronics Engineering Technology program at a local Philadelphia technical school. That was when the likelihood of being drafted regularly filled my thoughts, thanks to one of my classmates. Of all the guys in my class, the two I was the friendliest with were Mel Timmons and Marty Arcaro, mainly because we were closest in age. They were the only military veterans in the group—the others were fresh out of high school. Mel had done four years in the Navy and Marty was in the Army Reserves after having put in his six months of active duty. While they both teased everyone in the class that we were all headed for Vietnam as soon as we graduated, I became the main target of Marty's constant taunting. Every chance he got he reminded me that his active duty service was behind him but mine lay ahead, and Vietnam was where I was going to wind up. "Uncle Sam's gonna get you," he would say, with a finger pointing at my nose. I always shrugged it off, but he would give me a twisted, devilish grin and laughingly say, "You'll see, Howard, Sam's gonna get your ass, you'll see. And then it'll be off to 'Nam for you." I tried not to let him get to me, but I knew what he said could certainly happen. As long as I was in school I had a student deferment from the draft, but as soon as I graduated it would be reclassified to a non-exempt status. And with each passing month the fighting in Vietnam escalated and our military presence increased, making Marty's prediction all the more likely.

I was given Judy's name and number by a friend of hers, who also happened to be a cousin of mine, a few months after the program started, and after a few lengthy phone conversations we had our first date. We hit it off from the start, and were married four months before graduation. She has always said it was love at first sight, and firmly believed we were destined for each other—that fate brought us together, that spending our lives together was predetermined. Up until my tour in Vietnam, I would never have considered fate to be an influencing factor in my life, but when I look back at some of the things that happened, or more notably didn't happen to me there, I have come to believe there must be something to it. We spent our honeymoon at a resort that catered to newlyweds, during which we became pretty friendly with a Canadian couple. On our last day together the husband insisted we take their phone number and get in touch with them if we ever got to Toronto. Seeing them again seemed unlikely, but we thanked them for the invitation and took off for our tiny three-room apartment, our jobs, and my remaining few months of school. I never would have thought that less than a year later we would be with them in Canada discussing something that could affect the rest of our lives.

A week after graduation I began a new job as an IBM Customer Engineer; that's a fancy title for a computer technician. An IBM employment recruiter had come to the school about a month prior to determine who in my class, if any, might get job offers. After undergoing a battery of tests, I was thrilled to be one of only two who met IBM's high standards. And when the job was offered I accepted without hesitation. I was on cloud nine. I was a very happy, newly-married, 23-year-old starting out on a new career with the most prominent computer company in the country. I bought my first new car—a 1966 Pontiac Tempest—to celebrate. Life was good.

Less than six months later, however, all that changed when a letter arrived that would thrust me into the most perilous time of my life. It was a warm spring day and I couldn't wait to tell Judy how pleased my manager was when he found out I fixed a problem that had eluded two of his top CEs for days. But when I walked into our apartment that evening, instead of being greeted by a smiling face and a lingering kiss, I found her sitting hunched over on the couch, sobbing nonstop, her eyes red and puffy, and her face drained of color. My immediate thought was that someone in the family must be seriously ill or injured, maybe even dead. Judy didn't say a word; still sobbing, she just looked up, and with a trembling hand gave me the tear-stained letter she had been clutching. It was an induction notice from my local draft board, instructing me to report to the Philadelphia Military Induction Center on April 17th, 1967. I had been drafted. Even though I knew all along that it could happen, it still came as a shock. My life had never been better, and Marty wasn't around to keep reminding me of the possibility, so I really didn't give it much thought. I broke out in a cold sweat, my heart started pounding, my head began to throb, and questions immediately began swirling around in my mind. What'll happen now? What can I do? Is there any way I can get out of this? Who would know? Who could I call? I had lots of questions, but not a single answer. Suddenly a picture of Marty popped into my head, a big grin on his face, and his finger inches from my nose. I could almost hear him laughing at me and saying: "See Howard, it's exactly like I said it would be—Uncle Sam's got you and your ass is grass. Vietnam, here you come."

Before I got drafted, I never thought of myself as being either a hawk or a dove regarding our involvement in Vietnam. I wasn't a pacifist but neither was I gung-ho about the war. I really didn't have much opinion one way or the other. It wasn't as though we were attacked like we were at Pearl Harbor. If that had happened I probably would have voluntarily enlisted, but of course that wasn't the case. The World War II and Korean War movies I saw on TV and in movie theaters were exciting to watch and they definitely stimulated a lot of patriotism, but never enough to make me want to be a soldier. I never handled a real firearm of any kind, only plastic guns and cap pistols, and I was far from the rugged outdoor type. I wasn't a hunter, not much of a fisherman, and my one and only overnight experience in the woods was when I was a Cub Scout. After spending a shivering night sharing a lumpy sleeping bag with little crawling things, I parted ways with the Scouts and camping forever. No matter how I looked at it, I simply could not picture myself in the army, not in any capacity, let alone being in actual combat. Just thinking about having to kill another human being was nerve-wracking enough, but even worse was the thought of facing an enemy soldier and *not* being able to pull the trigger. Suddenly my life didn't seem so good after all.

Chapter 3 – To Go or Not To Go

Judy and I were up all night trying to think of how I might get out of it, but we kept coming up empty. I was in good health, didn't have any political connections, couldn't go back to school, and it was too late to get into the reserves or the National Guard. While I didn't ask, I wondered if my fatalist wife thought this new twist in our lives was also meant to be. Even if it was fate, I kept asking myself *why me*? None of my friends or relatives got drafted, just me. Why didn't any of them, why only me?

The next morning I went to see my manager at IBM and gave him the news, which didn't seem to have much of an effect on him at all. He didn't seem at all concerned about losing a newly hired, newly trained technician from his already shorthanded staff, but maybe he just figured there was no point in getting upset over something he had no control of. He said there was a slim chance I could be given a deferment because of IBM being a major contractor that provided computer equipment for the war effort, and he would see what could be done. I didn't get my hopes up, so I was not surprised when he let me know a few days later there would be no deferment. All the company was able to do was to get me a one-month postponement, which gave me a new reporting date of May 15th. During those next few weeks Judy and I halfheartedly made arrangements to cancel our apartment lease and move what little furniture we had into her parent's house. I continued working through the end of April, and my manager said my job would be waiting for me when I returned. Judy took a two-week vacation from her job, and we decided to get away for a week before I had to leave.

We left for Niagara Falls the first week in May and found a quiet motel within walking distance of the American Falls. It was very picturesque and the weather was perfect, but with our separation looming it was much less enjoyable than it otherwise could have been. After a few days of sightseeing on the U.S. side we decided to check out the Canadian Falls. What surprised me, with so many young Americans going to Canada specifically to dodge the draft and the war in Vietnam, was how easily we breezed across the border without so much as a single question asked of us. Perhaps it was because Judy was with me, but even if that was the case, I think our border patrol agents should have done more than casually glance at our driver licenses and wave us across. I wondered why we even bothered to put guards on our border if all they did was act like bored traffic cops. It made me think our government didn't care about the large number of draft dodgers leaving the country. Maybe they really didn't, since there was still an almost unlimited supply of eligible young men in the draft pool to draw from.

After another few days we had enough of the Canadian side as well, but before heading home we remembered the invitation from the Toronto couple we met on our honeymoon. We gave them a call and upon hearing how close we were they immediately invited us to spend a day or two at their house. We arrived late in the afternoon, and after settling in and exchanging small talk, we went to a quaint little French restaurant in downtown Toronto for dinner. When I told them about my job with IBM and my getting drafted the husband asked if I was looking forward to my military service. I answered with a resounding *no*, but added that there didn't seem to be any way to avoid it. With a very serious expression on his face, he said: "Howard, don't be crazy. You're already here in Canada so why not just stay? I'm a lawyer and my firm has done a lot of legal work for IBM Canada, and I'm absolutely certain I can get you a job with them tomorrow. You could be doing the exact same type of work here that you've been doing with IBM in the states. You would have a good job, a good salary, and no worries about having to go to Vietnam. The Canadian government won't allow you to be dragged back and you can stay right here with us until you get situated." It was pretty obvious by what he said that he was not a supporter of the war, in fact, just the opposite.

But what he said took me completely by surprise. It was no secret that Canada had become a safe haven for thousands of draft dodgers, but even when I thought about that as we crossed the border, it never entered my mind to become one of them. Abandoning my country seemed just as unlikely to me as volunteering for the army, but after hearing how easy it would be for him to get me a job with IBM Canada I found myself thinking it was at least worth considering. And that's what I spent that entire night doing; lying in bed, fully awake, and thinking of nothing else. Once again my mind was filled with questions. If I stayed in Canada would I have to give up my U.S. citizenship? If so, was that worth avoiding military service and the probability of going to Vietnam? But, slim as it was, there was the possibility I might not even get sent to Vietnam. An even if I did, I might end up in some type of a non-combat position. In fact, the army has a lot of IBM computers in Vietnam, and since I'm already an experienced technician it's possible I could wind up working in that type of job. But what if I wound up in the infantry? I could get wounded, maybe crippled for life, or worse, I could die. I was going around in circles, totally overwhelmed, and Judy offered no help whatsoever. She actually surprised me when she said she would stand by me and support me no matter what I decided, but the decision had to be mine, and mine alone.

Staying in Canada was very tempting. It would eliminate those fears immediately, but it wouldn't be like taking a temporary job for a few years. If I knew I would only be there until the war was over and could return to the states with no repercussions I might have leaned more in that direction. But that, of course, wasn't the case. Staying meant deserting my country, giving up my U. S. citizenship, and actually becoming a Canadian. All night long I bounced back and forth. The safest choice was to stay right there, even though Judy and I might never see our families again, even though I would forever be called a draft dodger, even though we would no longer be Americans. I wondered if I would be able to tell the kids we planned to have why all their ancestors were Americans, but *they* were Canadians. They would find out anyway, and what would they think of me when they did? To stay may have been the safer choice, but that didn't make it the easiest.

Before I was able to answer my own questions, I started thinking about Judy's fatalistic attitude toward life. I knew she thought it was fate that I got drafted, so if my death was already predestined, it shouldn't matter whether I stayed in Canada or retuned home. If it was my destiny to die within the next two years it would happen no matter where I might be—whether in a Vietnam jungle or stepping off a Canadian sidewalk. I wanted something concrete to help me decide, yet fate was the only thing I was able to come up with to steer me in what I hoped was the right direction. But would it? Some would say it was fate that brought us to Canada, so we should just stay. That made a lot of sense, and for a while I began to think it might be the path I should take. And Judy's willingness to stay if that was what I decided was pushing me even further toward remaining there. But at the same time, it left me with a very empty feeling. If I didn't return to the United States I felt there would always be a void in my life, as though a part of me was missing. That was a pretty perplexing thought, and I was fearful I wouldn't be able to live with that.

I was faced with an unsure future no matter what decision I made, and there was no one I could turn to for help. Judy was right, the decision had to be mine alone to make. In spite of my fear of Vietnam and my fear of dying, I realized there was no way I could knowingly desert my country. I could not be a draft dodger in spite of what might lie ahead. I had to return home. I think Judy was even more fearful about my going to war than I was, but when I told her my decision I could tell she was relieved that we would not be staying in Canada. At breakfast, I thanked our friend for his offer to help and we left for Philadelphia later that morning.

My last night at home was spent lying awake with Judy snuggled up next to me, staring at the ceiling, wondering what my future would be like. I tried to stay positive, forcing myself to focus on coming back to Judy intact and unharmed, even if I got sent to Vietnam. But as hard as I tried I couldn't stop the negative thoughts from sneaking in. If I was as much a fatalist as Judy I probably would have taken more of a *what-will-be-will-be* attitude. But I hadn't advanced to her level of belief in destiny, so all I did was get myself worked up to an even greater level of fear and anxiety. I was out of bed and dressed well before dawn, but hardly ready for what I was facing. I hadn't eaten much the day before so I should have been hungry, but just thinking about food made me feel queasy. The butterflies in my stomach felt more like a flock of birds, with their wings flapping away. Breakfast was a gulp of orange juice and two cups of coffee, which did nothing to settle my stomach.

We went to the induction center in my dad's car, my parents in the front seat, Judy and I in the back, wrapped in each other's arms. No one said a word. We had already said all there was to say many times over. We arrived early, my dad parked the car alongside the curb, and we all just sat there quiet and motionless until it was time for me to go. At eight o'clock, after hugs, kisses and teary goodbyes on the sidewalk, I nervously turned away and walked toward the building entrance. A part of me wanted to turn around, jump back into the safety of my father's car, and get the hell away from there as fast as possible—back to Toronto. But I couldn't let that happen. I had made my decision and I was sticking to it. As Judy would say, I was in fate's hands.

I entered the center with my induction letter in hand and was directed to the end of a long line of guys waiting to check in. From there, it was into the processing room, a large open area with numbered desks on one side and doors leading to smaller rooms on the opposite side. The whole morning was spent moving slowly from one processing station to the next, filling out forms, answering questions, undergoing basic physical and mental exams, including hearing and eye tests. I was given multiple inoculations, administered simultaneously in both arms with special air guns. At the finance desk I was told I would be receiving all of $96 a month, plus free clothing, free medical care, and free room and board, all compliments of Uncle Sam. I guess all those freebies were supposed to make me feel appreciative, but they didn't, not even a little.

After all the forms, exams, and medical evaluations were done, those of us not rejected for physical or psychological reasons were herded into an auditorium and told to remain standing. A few minutes later an army officer walked up to the podium, told us to raise our right hands, and then had us repeat an oath to defend and protect our country and Constitution. Then a burly sergeant wearing fatigues and a Smokey Bear hat went to the podium, called out about two dozen names from the two or three hundred of us, and directed them to the rear of the room. As they were escorted out by two other muscular sergeants, they were given the shocking news that they were on their way to Parris Island for Boot Camp—they had just become United States Marines. The rest of us were in the army and would be going to Fort Bragg, North Carolina for our Basic Training. My head was buzzing with the same questions that kept me awake the night before. What would the next two years be like? Could I stay out of danger? Would I come back under my own power or in a box with a flag draped over it? What did fate have in store for me? My stomach started doing flip-flops and I made it to a men's room just in the nick of time. Sitting on the toilet, my heart was pounding, my chest felt tight, I couldn't stop my hands from shaking, and a lump in my throat made it hard to breathe. I thought I might be having a heart attack, but after a while the pounding and shaking eased up enough for me to breathe easier, so I figured it was just nerves getting the best of me. I know now it was a panic attack, but back then I had never even heard the term *panic attack.* I left the stall, splashed water on my face, and slowly made my way back to the auditorium. My stomach was still fluttering, my legs were a little wobbly, and I was very apprehensive about my future, but I knew I would have to find a way to deal with my fears. I had to accept the fact that I was in the army and would probably wind up in Vietnam, so I better make sure I do everything possible to become the best damn soldier I could be if I hoped to survive the next two years.

Chapter 4 – Basic Training

My two years began with getting my head shaved, having my picture taken for my ID card, and being issued a new set of clothes; two sets of fatigues, army green underwear, t-shirts, socks, and a pair of combat boots. Following that was push-ups, marching, more push-ups, running, and still more push-ups. "Give me twenty" were words I never want to hear again, ever. Then came a day of testing to determine what MOS (Military Occupation Specialty) I would be assigned. I wasn't surprised that I got high scores in electronics, but very surprised that I also scored high in leadership skills, which led to being offered the opportunity to go to OCS (Officer Candidate School). Since I had no leadership or management experience whatsoever, it was quite unexpected. If I accepted, I would have been commissioned a Second Lieutenant upon completing the program, and would be required to serve two years starting from that point. Since it took ten months to go from Basic Training through OCS, it meant spending an additional ten months in the army. Had I not been married I probably would have accepted, but there was no way I wanted to be away from Judy even ten days more than I had to, so I respectfully turned it down.

Because of my high electronics scores the sergeant reviewing my results said he was going to recommend me for an RTO (Radio Telephone Operator) MOS, which really has nothing at all to do with electronics. An RTO is the guy who carries a two-way radio on his back for his unit leader when in the field. I told him that since I was already a trained computer technician, the army could put me to work in that capacity without the need for any further training, so that's what I thought he should recommend me for. He took me by complete surprise when he handed me the MOS book that listed all the specialties and said if I could find that specific MOS he would put me in for it. In a matter of minutes I found the one that was an exact match to an IBM CE and I watched him write that code in the appropriate box on my paperwork. I left the testing building feeling pretty good about my prospects of landing a computer job, but that jubilant feeling only lasted until shortly before the Basic Training program was scheduled to end. That's when I found out my assigned MOS was 11B, Light Weapons Infantryman. I always wondered if he really put me in for the computer position or if he just tore up the papers and rewrote them with an infantry recommendation. There's also the possibility that it was because I turned downed OCS. It always amazed me that the army would take guys who were already trained and experienced in specialized fields and put them into totally different jobs that required a lot of new training. And at the same time they would take guys with absolutely no technical knowledge whatsoever and spend thousands of dollars training them for high-tech jobs. I assume there is some military rationale for those decisions, but I seriously doubt they would make any logical sense to anyone outside the military hierarchy.

Basic Training was just as the words imply, training in basic army skills, such as the use of rifles, hand guns, machine guns, hand grenades and bayonets, as well as rudimentary hand-to-hand combat. We did a lot of marching, a lot of running, and lots of pushups. I wasn't in the best of physical shape when Basic started, but as the weeks went by I continued to get stronger and better able to do all that was required. To qualify for graduation we had to be proficient in weapons use and pass a physical fitness test that included push-ups, sit-ups, pull-ups, a long-distance run, and the low crawl—crawling fifty yards under concertina wire with a rifle across our arms and live bullets being fired above the wire. I passed them all well above the minimum requirements.

It wasn't easy to get used to some of the army's methods designed to break down the individuality of new recruits and get everyone to work together as a team. I experienced the first of those methods as soon as we were assigned to a barracks—the arrangement of the bathroom facilities, although I never understood how it helped develop comradeship between the men. The urinals were lined up on one wall and toilets on the opposite wall, with no dividers separating any of them. Open urinals were very common in the 60's, as they still are today, but even then, toilets in public bathrooms were always separated by some kind of dividers. The only other things on that side of the bathroom were rolls of what became commonly know as *John Wayne* toilet paper: *It's rough, it's tough, and it doesn't take shit off of anyone.* But little by little I adapted to the lifestyle changes and the new challenges I faced as a soldier.

The only real issue I had during Basic was the extra harsh treatment I received from my DI (Drill Instructor). Making sure new recruits are in good physical shape is obviously an important part of the training, as is the mental conditioning they undergo. The objective is to prepare the men for actual combat, where lives depend on following orders without hesitation and being physically able to carry them out. I agreed with the philosophy, but as to implementation, only up to a point, and I had already been pushed well beyond that limit. One particularly hot and humid day we were practicing rifle drills, and no matter how well I did my DI insisted otherwise, which resulted in my getting pulled out of ranks so he could torment me in front of the whole platoon. As I stood there with my arms straight out in front of me, he laid my M-14 rifle across my arms, with orders not to let my arms drop below shoulder level. The M-14, unloaded, with no magazine, weighs just over nine pounds. That's not much under normal circumstances, but it feels much heavier when it's resting across outstretched arms. Every time my arms began to lower under the weight, the sergeant screamed derogatory words and phrases about me, my family, and my heritage. After some twenty minutes of this abuse, I found myself thinking those infamous words of Popeye the Sailor Man right before he poured a can of spinach into his mouth: *"I yams what I yam* and *I've had all I can stands. I can't stands no more."*

I slowly put my rifle down on the ground, stood next to it in the *at-ease* position, and very respectfully informed my sergeant that I had enough. I would do all that was normally required, but I refused to be part of his over-the-top tactics. For at least ten minutes he screamed louder than before, threatening to have me recycled, even threatened me with a court martial and a Bad Conduct Discharge. I remained at-ease and simply responded to his tirade with a *do-whatever-you-have-to-do* attitude. At that moment I really didn't give a damn what he did, even if it meant getting booted out of the army. In the end, he told me to pick up my rifle and rejoin the ranks, and then he had the platoon continue the drills. To my surprise, nothing happened at all. He actually left me alone from that moment on. No more harassment, no extra work, no making examples of me, no more threats. No repercussions whatsoever.

A few days after that incident, we were awakened earlier than normal and asked who had driver's licenses and knew how to drive a stick shift. I had been told many times that it was not wise to volunteer for an unknown detail, but being groggy and not fully awake, I did just that. Two of us did, in fact, and we were ordered to get dressed, grab a quick breakfast, and report to the duty officer at the Motor Pool. After a few hours of driver training on jeeps and small trucks, followed by a driving test, we were issued military driver's licenses. From that time on, whenever we had to be driven to one of the training sites, I was assigned to drive one of the trucks used to transport the men. Occasionally I would even serve as an officer's jeep driver instead of pulling KP or some other distasteful job. Apparently, there are times when volunteering actually turns out to be a good move. Was this simply a case of pure chance, or could it have been a reward for putting up with my DI's bullshit for so long? Did the hand of fate play a role? I'll never know, but I can make a few guesses.

Chapter 5 – Infantry Training

On the final day of Basic Training, I was promoted to Private/E-2 and given orders to report to Fort Jackson, South Carolina for Infantry AIT (Advance Individual Training). It was official; my MOS was 11B, Light Weapons Infantryman. Infantry AIT was designed to pick up where Basic left off, focusing on the skills needed to be a combat-ready soldier. During the Vietnam War it had been modified to go beyond what the program previously consisted of, with more time spent on weaponry and hand-to-hand combat, and special emphasis on jungle warfare. Weapons training involved the M-14 and M-16 rifles, M-60 machine gun, M-79 grenade launcher and the M-1911, a .45-caliber handgun. Prior to entering the army, I never handled any kind of firearms, so I was very surprised that I scored as high as I did on the rifles and handgun. In fact, I scored high in all areas of the training, in spite of the one unexpected problem that occurred during one of our marches, I sprained my ankle.

In addition to daily PT (Physical Training) and a lot of running, AIT included regular *forced marches*. We would often march as much as ten miles with full packs, steel helmets, and rifles. Some were during the day and some at night, alternating between wooded trails and blacktop roads. It was on one of the road marches late in the training that I took a spill and injured my ankle. There were always at least three or four DIs on the marches, one leading the column, one bringing up the rear, and one or more in the middle, trying to keep us evenly spaced and moving at a uniform pace. That wasn't easy to do as some guys always tired easily and slowed down the rest of the column. When that happened, the DIs would scream at everyone falling behind to run and close the gap to the men ahead. That particular morning we were on the last leg of a ten-mile march that started well before daybreak. It was still fairly dark and I was in the middle of a group that kept falling behind. Even a small gap was more than enough reason to get the DIs shouting for us to speed it up and close ranks. But as I ran to catch up, my right foot came down on the very edge of the blacktop, which was a couple of inches higher than the ground next to the road. As a result, my ankle twisted and I fell onto the ground. My body was okay, but not the ankle.

We always had a medic with us on our marches, and as this was a road march, he was bringing up the rear in a jeep that had been converted to a mini infirmary on wheels. When the jeep got to me the medic wiggled my ankle around, told me no bones appeared to be broken, and suggested I go to the base infirmary if it still bothered me after I finished the march. No ride back—just finish the march. However, when he saw I was doing more hobbling than walking, let alone running, he decided it was best to drive me back after all. When I arrived at the barracks and took my boot off my ankle immediately swelled to the size of a grapefruit, forcing me to hop to the infirmary on one foot. The doctor agreed with the medic; there didn't seem to be any broken bones, more than likely it was just a minor sprain. He wrapped the ankle in an ace bandage, gave me a few aspirins, and put me on a light-duty medical profile for a few days. The swelling did eventually subside enough for me to get my boot on, but never totally. I kept returning to the infirmary and kept getting told the same thing—my ankle was fine and I was okay for normal duty. I knew if I kept complaining I would wind up getting recycled, which wasn't very appealing. I had already been through the toughest part of the training and didn't want to have to do it all over again, especially if the ankle continued to bother me. I made sure to have plenty of aspirin with me at all times, kept my ankle wrapped and my boot laced up as tight as possible, and I managed to keep up with the rest of the men during the remainder of the training.

As the end of AIT approached, I expected orders for 'Nam, of course, but didn't have a clue as to what unit I would be assigned. And the nagging thoughts of getting wounded or killed were always on my mind, as was the case with all the guys in my training company—except for Harry. From the time we started AIT, Harry kept telling everyone that he would find a way to keep from going to Vietnam. Some how, some way he was determined to stay in the States. He thought about going AWOL (Absent-With-Out-Leave), which was not that uncommon, but he was afraid of getting caught and winding up in jail. His only alternative was to come up with a way to injure himself badly enough to get a medical discharge, or at least get assigned to a non-combat job. Eventually he came up with a plan: he would get drunk and have someone break one of his legs. And just a few nights after telling us his plan, that's exactly what he did. He drank a pint of whiskey and sat back in a chair in one of the empty barracks with one leg stretched out on the seat of another chair. He closed his eyes and waited for his paid accomplice to jump on his leg from an upper bunk. And it worked as expected. The impact of a 200-pound man jumping feet-first from six feet above onto his knee immediately shattered his kneecap. We didn't find out about it until the next morning when we realized Harry hadn't been in his bunk all night. He wasn't anywhere in the barracks either, but we later heard that he wound up in the hospital. I don't know what story he made up, and I never did find out if he got his discharge, but such a severe injury must have kept him out of Vietnam.

Chapter 6 – NCO School

I was well aware that casualties in Vietnam had been steadily increasing among the NCO (Non Commissioned Officer) ranks, but I was unaware that a number of specialized NCO training schools had been set up to help alleviate the shortage of combat sergeants. The program was designed to produce "Buck Sergeants" (the lowest sergeant rank) similar to how OCS produces Second Lieutenants, with a much greater emphasis on jungle warfare and tactics than AIT provided. Unlike OCS, however, no additional time in service was required. Of all the men in my AIT company, I was the only one selected for the program, with no option to decline. NCO School was where I was being sent, whether I wanted to go or not. Had I been given a choice I'm sure I would have accepted it anyway, as it meant an automatic promotion to Corporal E-4 when the training started, and a promotion to Sergeant E-5 upon completion. Of course the pay was higher and there were some additional privileges, but most important was that I would be able to live off base with Judy for the duration of the program. Given a choice, it would have been a no-brainer.

Many of the career sergeants began using terms like *Instant NCO*, *Shake 'n' Bake*, and *Whip-n-Chills* to identify the noncoms that the NCO program produced. They complained that it took years to develop a skilled and capable non-commissioned officer, and this new training program was all wrong, it couldn't possibly turn out effective sergeants in such a short period of time. But the army's

NCO schools were designed to do one thing and one thing only—in one military branch, for duty in one place in the world—to create fire-team and squad leaders who would be effective in Vietnam—period. It didn't cover the many duties or responsibilities required of NCOs in non-combat assignments or during peacetime. The army needed more combat-ready sergeants quickly in Vietnam, and this was what they put in place to make that happen, in spite of the complaints from veteran NCOs.

The program was split into two major segments. The first, taught by Vietnam veterans and Army Rangers, was 12 weeks of intensive hands-on training, broken down into three parts:
(1) physical conditioning, hand-to-hand combat, weapons, first aid, map reading, communications, and indirect fire control;
(2) instruction in effective platoon, squad, and fire-team tactics; (3) a *dress rehearsal* for Vietnam—a full week of patrols, ambushes, defensive perimeters, and navigation, all conducted in simulated, but very realistic, Vietnam environments.

The second segment was 10 weeks of practical application of leadership skills by serving as assistant leaders in training centers or unit Squad Leaders with Infantry AIT Training Companies.

The army had established three training sites for this program and I was assigned to the East Coast location at Fort Benning, Georgia, with a week of travel time to get there. I took the first flight I could get to Philadelphia and was able to spend a few days there before Judy and I had to leave for Georgia. Judy had a real surprise waiting for me when I got home—she was pregnant. It was the result of a Labor Day weekend together near the end of AIT, which put her due date around the last week of May. I was thrilled at the thought of becoming a father, yet I couldn't help being nervous about it. A quick calculation told me I would be leaving for Vietnam weeks before the birth of my son or daughter, with no way to know if I would make it back for his or her first birthday. Needless to say that was not a pleasant thought; it took much of the joy out of Judy's news. I hardly got any sleep the next few nights thinking about how unfair it was to bring a child into the world knowing there was a strong possibility he or she would be fatherless. But we certainly didn't plan for this to happen. Or did we? I didn't, but what about Judy? I never asked her about that. Could she have consciously wanted to get pregnant just in case I didn't come back to her? I knew it was not uncommon during wartime—a wife or girlfriend wanting to be sure she would have a part of her loved one with her always. Or, maybe it was done subconsciously. In either case, I didn't want to say or do anything that might put a damper on the happiness Judy was feeling, so I said nothing.

One of the first things I did almost immediately after arriving at Fort Benning was to pay a visit to the base infirmary and get my bad ankle checked out again. The swelling had never subsided completely and it was uncomfortable, especially when I had to do a lot of running or marching. An x-ray finally confirmed there were no broken bones, just a very bad sprain. The infirmary doctor prescribed a series of whirlpool treatments at the base hospital, and the nurse in charge was able to schedule them without interfering with my training schedule. After completing the treatments with no significant improvement, the doctor gave me a cortisone injection, even though he wasn't overly optimistic that it would reduce either the swelling or the discomfort. When I asked him what else was available if the cortisone didn't help, he was very evasive. He said we would just have to wait to see how it was in a week or so. And as I suspected, the injection did no good at all. But I didn't want to drop out of the program, so I kept my ankle wrapped and again managed to put up with the pain for the rest of my training.

As for the actual training, I thought the program did a good job of preparing me for Vietnam and the responsibilities of a squad leader, although I only had AIT to compare it with. It wasn't until I got to 'Nam, however, that I appreciated exactly how good it really was. Quite a bit of time was spent on developing leadership skills, but the largest portion was devoted to fighting a jungle war; how to survive and lead an effective fighting force against guerilla warfare. We played many very realistic war games in heavily wooded areas and in simulated villages typical of what we would encounter in Vietnam. Among other things, we went on patrols through dense woods, many for days at a time; learned how to read maps, set up ambushes, and call in artillery and air support. We climbed walls, climbed trees, waded through streams and deep creeks, stayed out for days in the middle of heavy rainstorms, dug a lot of foxholes, and learned how to live off the land. Rattlesnake meat does taste a lot like chicken. We rappelled out of hovering helicopters from 30 to

50 feet above the ground, and jumped out of the choppers from about six feet while they were still moving.

I graduated from the first part of the NCO program with a promotion to the rank of sergeant and my MOS was upgraded to 11B40; the 40 indicating an E-5 grade sergeant. It was a Friday afternoon and my orders were to report back to Fort Jackson, South Carolina the very next Monday for the second phase of the program. I was assigned as a squad leader in an infantry AIT company, and for the next ten weeks my job was much like that of an assistant drill instructor. I took orders from my DI and did everything I could to get my squad functioning well above and beyond minimum performance levels. With a few weeks to go, I returned to the base infirmary to get my ankle re-evaluated. This time around I got a doctor who thought my original sprain was severe enough that the ankle should have been immobilized with a cast immediately after the injury. Although he wasn't too optimistic, he felt that putting me in a cast even at that late date might be helpful. When I got back to our apartment, Judy was surprised to see me hobbling up the steps with my leg in a cast from my toes to just below the knee. The cast had a round rubber piece on the bottom that enabled me to walk on it without the need for crutches or a cane, but I wasn't allowed to get it wet. That meant taking showers with my leg tightly wrapped in a plastic bag. The majority of my squad's training was finished so it didn't affect my status in the program, but I don't know if that was good or bad. I might have stayed out of Vietnam if I wasn't able to complete the training as scheduled. On the other hand, I could have gone anyway and might not have come back. Perhaps it was fate guiding me once again.

I received my orders for Vietnam at the completion of NCO school. After a 30-day leave, I was to report to the processing center at Oakland Army Base in California. Getting home however was a little complicated, as the cast made driving a bit awkward. Judy was about to enter her ninth month of pregnancy and was under doctor's orders to fly home, not to travel by car. Her doctor at the Fort Jackson hospital felt the drive from South Carolina to Philadelphia would be too much for her in the condition she was in. We arranged for her to fly back to Philly, leaving me to pack the car and make the drive back myself. But because of the cast, my sister Julie flew down to make the drive back with me. I picked her up at the airport and, after packing the car, we took off. As it turned out I wound up doing all the driving, but having her along for company certainly made the drive easier than it otherwise would have been.

Chapter 7 – Home on Leave

I had to be in Oakland on May 12th, and from there it would be off to Vietnam. Judy's due date was about two weeks after I was to leave, and she and our baby would be staying with her parents while I was gone. Just prior to our getting back to Philly her father suffered a heart attack. We were told it was a mild one that wouldn't have any long-term effects, and when we got back he did seem to be recuperating fairly well. However, only a few days later he suffered another, far more serious, attack. It was life-threatening.

When Judy saw her doctor later that week he didn't foresee any complications with the delivery as long as she was able to keep calm and relaxed through the remaining weeks. But the double whammy of her father's critical condition and my leaving gave the doctor serious concerns about the effects of the anxiety she was experiencing, not only on her but also on our unborn child. He wrote a letter detailing why he believed it was a medical necessity for me to remain home with Judy until after the baby was born. The next day I went to Fort Dix Army Base in New Jersey, presented my orders and the doctor's letter, and requested a 30-day emergency medical leave. Surprisingly, the leave was granted on the spot, making June 7th my new date to be in Oakland.

The extension was a blessing for us. Knowing I would be there when our child was born eased much of the anxiety we had both been experiencing. It also gave me a little more time to see if I could get another evaluation of my ankle. Valley Forge Army

Hospital was the closest army medical facility, so off I went in the hopes I could see a doctor without an appointment. Not only did I see a doctor, the Major who examined me was the head of the hospital's orthopedic department. He removed the cast, had X-rays taken, and gave me what seemed to be a pretty thorough exam. I wasn't expecting to hear anything different from what I had been told before, which was why I was surprised to hear him tell me the weakness and discomfort was because the ligaments around my ankle had become permanently stretched. He said the sprain was apparently severe enough that the first doctor I saw should have put the ankle in a cast immediately. If that had been done he was pretty certain I would have had a complete recovery. As it was, too much time had passed for the ligaments to return to normal, and they were not repairable. The weakness in the ankle was something I would have to live with for the rest of my life.

What surprised me even more was the doctor's assessment that the weakness in my ankle was severe enough to get my MOS reclassified and probably get me transferred out of the infantry. That took a moment to sink in, and when it did my immediate thought was that maybe, just maybe, I might not go to Vietnam after all. I couldn't believe my ears when I heard him say almost the same words I was just thinking. Not only shouldn't I be in the infantry, he said I probably should not be going to Vietnam in any capacity with that type of condition. My mind began to race. Maybe I could even wind up with a medical discharge. But those thoughts were immediately cut off when the doctor continued, "however, it's unfortunate for you that I'm going to Vietnam in a few weeks myself, and because of that I'll be damned if I'm going to be the one to stop anyone else going over there." I stood there dumbfounded, wondering how he could say such a thing. He was a doctor, a medical professional. He had a responsibility to help people, not purposely put their lives in jeopardy. I was in such a daze I didn't even notice that he had already signed off on my paperwork, indicating I was fit for normal duty. He handed me the papers, said I was to report to Oakland as scheduled, turned, and left the room. For a minute I thought I must have misunderstood what he said, but one look at paperwork confirmed it. Of course, there was no mention of his real assessment of my condition; instead it simply said that my ankle was perfectly normal.

On the way home I was unsure if I should tell Judy what the doctor said. I didn't want to get her any more worked up than she already was, but at the last minute I decided to be up front with her—she should know exactly what happened. She wasn't expecting to hear good news, but she wasn't prepared for the doctor's outrageous remarks. We talked about reporting him to someone, but didn't know who to complain to or even if it would do any good. After all, he was the head of the hospital's orthopedic department, how much of a chance would I have going against him? At that moment I was more concerned about Judy and the baby than I was about me, and since she had begun to calm down and no longer seemed as upset about it, I let it drop. Her dad was home from the hospital and was beginning to make a slow but steady recovery. Her delivery date was getting closer and I would be there when our son or daughter was born, so her spirits were okay for the time being. A few nights later she started having contractions and by early morning they were coming pretty regularly, so we jumped in the car and took off for the hospital. It didn't take long to get there, and the way Judy had been complaining on the way, I thought it would be a pretty quick delivery. I could not have been more wrong. It was well over twelve hours after getting to the hospital when Ellen Lynn was born. It was Monday, May 27, 1968, at 9:37 p.m., and mother and daughter were doing fine.

I wanted to make the most of the short time I would have with them before I had to go, but I couldn't stop thinking about my episode with the doctor. And the more I did the angrier I got. With the recently gained knowledge of just how serious my injured ankle was, I decided to make one last-ditch effort to at least delay my leaving. I went to the hospital at the Philadelphia Navy Base hoping to get a navy doctor to concur with the army doctor and keep me from going to Vietnam. I did get to see a doctor in the orthopedic department and he was sympathetic, but said that even if he agreed with the other doctor he didn't have the authority to get my orders changed. His only suggestion was to put me back in a cast with the hope I could get seen by a doctor in Oakland and have better results there. I wasn't sure if I agreed with him, but after giving it all of a minute's thought, it was into a cast once again and then home to a surprised Judy.

Chapter 8 – Off To War

On June 6th I was at Philadelphia International Airport with Judy, Ellen, my parents, and my sister, waiting to board the plane to Oakland. After all the hugs, kisses, tears, and sad goodbyes once again, I hobbled onto the plane, my cast still on, and tried to relax as best I could. I was a new father going off to war with a cast on my leg, wondering if I would ever see my family again. And if I did make it home alive would I be in the same condition as when I left. What if I lost an arm or leg, or worse? What would happen if I got captured? Could I hold up to torture? I tried not to think about those things but stopping the thoughts was impossible. I tried to concentrate on all the good times I had with Judy but that did just the opposite—it only made me realize what I would be missing, especially Ellen's first year. Knowing I wouldn't be there when she said her first word, stood up for the first time, maybe even took her first steps only made me feel that much worse. I listened to music and tried reading a magazine but I couldn't even focus on the pictures. Nothing helped ease my misery.

The single-most unsettling thought was what would happen to Judy and Ellen if I died. The army provided a small amount of life insurance to widows of soldiers killed in action, which would not have lasted long. I also had to accept the fact that if I died Judy would eventually find someone else to fill her life. And if that were to happen I could only hope her new husband would not only make her happy, but be a good father to Ellen. That was comforting and troubling at the same time. If it came to pass and Judy did remarry, would her husband formally adopt Ellen? If so, would that mean her name would change? That was the most unsettling thought of all. Part of me said it would be good for her, but another part wanted Ellen to keep my name. Even if it were magically possible for her to remember me from our ten days together, there's no way she could ever know me, but I figured if she kept my name it would somehow keep us connected. So right then and there I took out a pen and paper and wrote a letter to Judy. I told her if I didn't make it back I wanted to be sure Ellen would keep my last name even if she was adopted. I tried as best I could to explain my reasoning, but I'm sure it didn't make as much sense to her as it did to me. It was one of the most difficult things I had ever done and I wasn't sure what effect it would have on Judy. I had a lot of second thoughts during the rest of the flight, but as the plane's wheels screeched when they touched down on the runway I was sure it was what I had to do. I mailed the letter as soon as I was able to buy a stamp and find a mailbox.

After calling Judy to tell her I landed okay, I got on an army shuttle bus to the base, found my way to the processing center and reported in. The first chance I got I was off to the infirmary about my ankle. I managed to see one of the doctors on duty but was told that unless I had a serious illness they did not have the authority to keep me there or change my orders. If anything was to be done it would have to wait until I got to Vietnam. Looking back, I often wonder if I left the cast on would it have kept me from being assigned to an infantry unit. But at the time all I could think of was how much more difficult it would be trying to stay alive in the middle of a war zone with a cast on my leg. So just before boarding the plane to Vietnam I went into a men's room and somehow managed to break the cast off, piece by piece.

The first full military divisions to arrive in Vietnam went as units by ship. Shortly thereafter most of the soldiers were sent in as individual replacements, not knowing what units they would be assigned to until they arrived. A few still went by boat and some were transported by military aircraft, but most were flown in by commercial airlines. My flight to Vietnam was on one of the commercial planes, a Boeing 707 operated by Continental Airlines. I don't know how many seats the plane had but every one was filled. It was mainly new replacements, but there were some soldiers and sailors going back for second tours. It was one of the quietest flights I was ever on. Even the guys returning to Vietnam didn't make much noise; they just seemed to be deep in thought like everyone else. Some men were reading, some were writing letters, but almost all the new replacements were staring expressionless into space. I'm not sure how many of those blank stares were coupled with silent prayers, but I suspect it was a lot. I know mine was, even though I was never very religious. I want to believe there is a God but it has always been difficult for me to believe in something on pure faith. While certain events in my life have given me hope that there is someone up there watching over me, there's no way I can know for sure—at least not as long as I am still alive.

Heading into a war zone, along with a couple of hundred soldiers, sailors and marines, on a commercial airplane, staffed by civilian pilots and stewardesses, was a strange experience. As a tray of typical airline food was handed to me I wondered if it would be my last good meal for quite a while. Even though airline food in the'60s was barely edible, I suspected it would be better than whatever I would be eating in Vietnam. The plane made one refueling stop in Hawaii and we were allowed to deplane and stretch our legs. As we left the plane we were ushered into a very large but simple waiting area away from the main terminal. There were seats, water fountains, vending machines, and rest rooms, but all the exit doors out of that room were locked. Obviously others used this stopover as a means of going AWOL, probably just merging into the crowds in the terminal. In any case, after about an hour we were escorted back onto the plane for the final leg of our journey. As quiet as the first half of the flight was, that last part was quieter still. There was no more reading and writing, just a bunch of teenagers and young men sitting there scared about what might lie ahead. Some had red, swollen eyes unable to hold back the tears; others occasionally could be heard sobbing softly above the silence. There was no talking, no eating, and no sleeping; it was as though everyone was in a trance. My eyes were closed, but my mind was fully awake, reliving as much of my jungle warfare training as possible. I wondered how prepared for combat I really was. Was it enough to keep me alive? Would I be able to lead a squad during a real battle? Could I pull the trigger when facing the enemy? I could only hope and pray that the answers were all *yes.*

The plane landed at Bien Hoa (pronounced Ben Wah) Air Base, about twenty miles north of Saigon City. It was one of a number of military replacement centers that were set up to process the troops entering and leaving the country. We taxied off the runway and came to a stop close to the processing building. A mobile stairway was pushed up to the plane, and as the plane's door opened my nostrils were bombarded by an intense, almost sickening stench, like nothing I had ever smelled before. At the same time, the air came alive with loud cheers and whistles from somewhere outside the plane. As I got to the open doorway, trying to figure out what that horrible smell was, the glare from the sunlight bouncing off the metal buildings made it almost impossible to keep my eyes open. It seemed ten times brighter than the afternoon sun on a hot summer day in Philadelphia. And within seconds of stepping into the open air my shirt was soaked, sweat was streaming down my face, and it was an effort just to breathe. I felt like I had just walked into a sauna with the temperature on the highest setting. I had experienced the heat and humidity of South Florida in mid-August, but that was like a warm spring morning compared to the extreme temperature and humidity that was assaulting my body. By the time I stepped off the stairway there wasn't a dry spot on my body—I felt like every pore was dripping sweat. I couldn't imagine how people functioned in such an oppressive climate, let alone fight a war, but I knew it wouldn't be long before I would find out firsthand.

Once my eyes were able to focus, I couldn't help but notice smoke filling the air. No matter what direction I faced, I saw huge plumes of black smoke coming from behind what looked like small wooden shacks. Actually they were more the size of the portable *Jiffy Johns* used today, except they weren't portable at all, they were one-person outhouses. I later found out the smoke and the horrible smell were byproducts of human shit being burned. The outhouses contained benches with holes in them, with the bottom half of 55-gallon drums beneath the holes. Throughout the day, the guys who were assigned to shit-burning detail would drag the drums out through hinged back doors, pour diesel fuel or gasoline into them, stir the mixture with a shovel or large paddle until the fuel and shit were well blended, and then set it on fire. Unless you have experienced it yourself it's impossible to know what a foul smell that creates. The best I can do to describe it is standing next to a large pile of fresh cow manure mixed with hot tar, and a fan blowing the smell into your face. As only the largest military bases in Vietnam had indoor plumbing, all the smaller bases used these disgusting, unsanitary, fly-infested outhouses, and burning was the only practical way to dispose of the human waste.

The piercing whistles and cheers that I heard were coming from men anxiously waiting for the plane to be cleaned and refueled so it could fly them out of Vietnam. All around the building were hundreds of men, some standing, some sitting, but all waiting for their *Freedom Bird* to fly them back to *The World*. Some were laughing and joking around with one another, mostly at our expense.

As we deplaned they called us the FNGs (Fuckin' New Guys), said half of us would be dead or wounded within a month, and the only way many of us would get out of Vietnam would be in body bags. I didn't think we would be greeted by a brass band, but this definitely wasn't the kind of welcoming committee I expected. Just being in Vietnam was frightening enough, but listening to taunts about body bags only added to my fear and anxiety.

As I continued looking around I couldn't help but notice some guys sitting alone, not cheering or whistling, not laughing, not even talking among themselves. They were just staring off into space with blank, lifeless expressions on their faces. It was almost as though they had lost something and didn't know where to start searching for it. The haunting, stone-faced, empty look I saw on so many faces that day, often called *the thousand-yard stare,* is fairly common among combat soldiers. The phrase was coined during the Second World War to describe the unfocused vacant gaze of battle-weary warriors attempting to block out the trauma of combat. But in all too many cases those unforgettable lingering memories we try so desperately to bury stay with us for the rest of our lives, and so does that thousand-yard stare. It's amazing how many combat vets can pick another combat warrior out of a crowd just by seeing that haunted look in his eyes, a look that never completely goes away. Unfortunately, only dead warriors have seen the end of war; those of us still alive have to live with our wars for the rest of our lives. And our faces reveal it. As the old country-western cliché goes: *you can take the boy out of the country, but you can't take the country out of the boy*. I believe the same holds true for combat veterans: *You can remove the soldier from the war, but you can't remove the war from the soldier.*

In the short time it took to cross the tarmac and get into the processing building my clothes were drenched in sweat and I was physically exhausted. As we entered, there was a mad rush for the water coolers. Even after gulping down a dozen cupfuls of water, I still was parched. The only things about in-processing that I remember clearly were presenting my orders to a clerk, turning in my U.S. money in exchange for MPCs (Military Payment Certificates), and getting assigned to my unit. MPCs were the only currency we were allowed to possess while in Vietnam, although American dollars were used openly throughout the country, especially in the black market. I arranged for all but $25 a month to be sent home to Judy. I was getting paid at an E-5 grade level, plus additional pay for overseas and combat duty, somewhere around $350 a month. After the paperwork was completed, all of us FNGs were taken outside and placed in groups based on our unit assignments. As one of the last to be called, I still had no idea where I was going until I heard the First Cavalry Division, followed by my name and one other. That did not make me happy; in fact, my anxiety level immediately jumped another few notches. Before arriving in 'Nam, I heard the only thing worse than being a Marine was being in the First Cav. Accurate or not, it was said that no other army infantry unit in Vietnam was as tough and gung-ho for action as the First Cavalry Division. It was also called the *First Air Cav* as it was the very first *Air Mobile* combat unit, making extensive use of helicopters for fire support and moving troops in and out of the field.

Before I knew it, I was on a C-130 cargo plane with the other First Cav replacement heading towards Camp Evans, the division headquarters. It was in Ahn Khe Province, on the eastern edge of what's known as the Central Highlands. Passenger accommodations on the plane were non-existent. All we had to sit on were fold down jump seats on each side of the cargo area, with single seat belts to prevent sliding off and banging into the cargo that totally filled the belly of the plane. After landing and reporting in, I was handed orders assigning me to E Company, First of the Fifth—1st Battalion, 5th Regiment. The only thing I was able to find out about Echo Company was that it was a newly formed unit, established just the previous month, May of 1968. Within an hour of landing at Evans I was back in the air, on a helicopter with mail and medical supplies, heading to Fire Base Barbara in Quang Tri (Qwang Tree) Province, just south of the DMZ—the Demilitarized Zone dividing North and South Vietnam.

Chapter 9 – Echo Recon

I reported in at E Company's operations tent and met the First Sergeant and Company Commander. I was told I would be a squad leader in the recon platoon, which consisted of only one squad led by Sergeant Jim Crouch. That squad would be split into two smaller ones, and I would be leading the second squad. A platoon normally had four squads, with the optimal size of a recon squad being six to eight men, although our numbers continually varied based on our changing manpower availability. As time went on, more men were assigned to the recon platoon and a third squad was formed. There was no fourth squad during E Company's first year of operation.

On paper, Echo Company was made up of three platoons—mortar, radar, and reconnaissance—although the recon platoon was the main operating unit. At that early stage of the company's existence, the mortar and radar platoons had only a few men in each and were essentially non-operational. The recon platoon's mission was threefold: (1) conduct reconnaissance missions in suspected enemy areas and gather as much information about the enemy as possible, (2) conduct squad and platoon-size ambushes, and engage any small enemy units we might encounter, and (3) serve as a ready-reaction force in the event one of the line companies needed assistance.

I met with Sgt. Crouch and found out I would be sharing a bunker with him, along with the local mosquitoes, ants, snakes, scorpions, mice, rats and other assorted unwanted critters. Scorpions liked to curl up in our boots, so making sure the boots were empty before putting them on was critical. Rats and mice would scamper around looking for food, even when we were in the bunkers. Whatever meager belongings we had, as well as any extra food and care packages from home, were stored in empty wooden ammo cases and small metal machinegun ammo boxes. Our beds were either ponchos or air mattresses that didn't stay inflated, and that was all that separated us from the dirt floors. There were a number of generators on the base but our bunkers were not among those that required electricity. If we needed light after dark it came from flashlights and candles.

My next stop was with the supply clerk, Bob Staab. I was issued an M-16 rifle, ammo clips and ammunition, bandoliers to hold the clips, a bayonet, a couple of canteens, a poncho, insect repellent, and one extra set of socks and underwear. The medic's tent was next, where I received a supply of anti-malaria and water purification tablets, both of which tasted so bad that many of the guys never used them. Side effects were not much fun either, the most common being diarrhea, usually mild but sometimes it was pretty severe. We had two medics assigned to our unit, Doc (Larry) Allin and Doc (Tom) McKay. Around the end of my first week with the company, I was given a present by a support sergeant who was scheduled to DEROS (Date Eligible to Return from Over Seas) in a few days—his .45 caliber pistol. Someone had given it to him shortly after he arrived in country, and since he couldn't take it with him because the serial numbers had been filed off he passed it on to me. And I passed it on to another new-in-country sergeant just before I left Vietnam.

Fire Base Barbara was a fairly large base on a flat hilltop that had been cleared of all trees and vegetation to accommodate the operations of the 1st of the 5th, which consisted of five Companies—A, B, C, D, E—along with air and artillery support groups. The helipad and artillery compounds were at opposite ends of the base, and the entire hilltop was surrounded by defensive bunkers. The bottom and sides of the hill were covered with concertina wire—a type of barbed wire—intended to prevent the enemy from making effective ground assaults against the base. Our bunkers were square or rectangular holes dug in the ground, usually about four feet deep. Sandbag walls extended three to four feet above ground, with openings for small windows and an entrance. Corrugated sheet metal was used for roofs, which was covered with five or six layers of sandbags for protection against enemy mortars and rockets.

As hot as it was in the open air it was at least ten degrees hotter inside the bunkers, which were filled with stagnant air and strong musty odors, except when it rained. And the rains, of course, often turned the dirt floors into mud. Many of the men slept on top of their bunkers, some hoping to find a little breeze, but most just trying to get away from our unwanted houseguests. Regardless of why they were sleeping in the open air, everyone would dive back inside whenever enemy mortars and rockets were fired at us, which was all too often. Incoming rockets gave off unique whistling sounds that usually gave us a few seconds warning of their deadly explosions. We never knew if the incoming barrage would be followed by a ground assault, which meant we always had to be fully prepared for one even before the mortars and rockets stopped. That's just one reason why I never went anywhere without my weapons and ammo. My .45 was always on me and my M-16 was never more than arms reach away.

Every once in a while during one of those attacks I would see an arm or a leg sticking out of one of the bunkers. The dangling limb belonged to a guy who was apparently so desperate to get out of the field that he was willing to get hit with a piece of shrapnel, even if it only gave him a short reprieve. The real hope was to get a non life-threatening wound, but serious enough to get sent back to the States. War affects some people in strange ways, ways they themselves would never have thought possible. At first, I found it hard to understand why someone would deliberately set himself up for the possibility of loosing an arm or leg, or worse. But as I soon found out first hand, regular exposure to the horrors of war, coupled with constant fear and anxiety, can screw up a person's mind big time.

In an attempt to keep Viet Cong and North Vietnamese sappers (specially trained assault troops) with satchel charges (small bags containing explosives) from sneaking through the wire, the base would hold a *Mad Minute* every night, but always at different times. For at least a solid minute, everyone on perimeter guard duty would set off flares, lob hand grenades, and fire rifles, machine guns, and grenade launchers down the hill. It was to keep the enemy unsure of the best time to launch an attack. Some nights there would be more than one mad minute, and of course, many nights guys would open up with sporadic gunfire when they saw shadows or heard noises down the hill. Usually when that happened other guys would fire as well, whether they had a target or not. That was safer than taking a chance the shadows or noises were not from the wind or animals, but from the enemy. Also, a noise coming from one side of the hill could just be a decoy for enemy soldiers trying to sneak up on us from a different side, so we had to be constantly alert and watchful. Some mornings we would find sections of the barbed wire cut open, and sometimes blood and torn clothing on the wire itself. Even though it was obvious at least one enemy soldier had been hit, we never once found a body on the hill. It's a pretty good bet we had wounded or killed some of them, but if so, their comrades carried them off during the night. Almost always, when a base camp did get overrun it was because one or more of the men on guard duty weren't doing their job. They had either fallen asleep or were goofing off. It's never easy to stay alert and focused in the dark for hours at a time, but not remaining vigilant can have deadly results, as too many men found out.

One side of the hill was designated as our trash dump. All the trash and garbage we generated was simply tossed onto the dump and periodically it was doused with gasoline and set on fire. Unfortunately, most of the rats that our garbage attracted made it out of the burning dump alive. They rummaged through the garbage during the day and all too often slept in our cozy bunkers at night. They definitely did *not* make very nice house pets. However, one of the guys did try to make a pet out of a monkey he caught, naming it Fritz. We also had a small black-and-white dog named Jude hanging around for a while, but one day he vanished, just like most of the dogs in South Vietnam. Apparently dog stew was a favorite delicacy of the local villagers, and I suspect that's where ours wound up.

The entire top of our hill was engulfed in an almost constant haze of smoke and dust. The smoke was from a combination of burning trash, burning shit, and exhaust fumes from trucks, jeeps, and helicopters. The dust was kicked up by the rotor blades of the choppers that constantly flew in and out of the base. The only time the haze and dust disappeared was when it was raining, but then the ground became a mini-swamp of puddles and mud. The only good thing about the rain was when it came down hard enough to fill the empty barrels we used for showers. We had make-shift wooden shower stalls with small platforms above them with 55-gallon drums sitting on the platforms to catch the rain water. With a ration of a few gallons per person, a barrel could accommodate showers for at least a dozen or more guys. It was refreshing, but that usually didn't last very long. After washing our bodies we almost always had to get back into the same ragged fatigues we wore day after day.

There was a mess tent on the base, but it was used mainly to feed the support personnel. Occasionally we got hot meals, but even when not in the field we ate mostly C-Rations. The C-Rats, as we called them, consisted of a few necessities in addition to the actual food. Each pack had a canned meat, canned fruit, canned bread or dessert, a snack, salt and pepper, instant coffee, powdered cream, chewing gum, a mini pack of four cigarettes, matches, a small roll of toilet paper, a spoon, and a P-38 mini can opener. The cans were from the 1940's, leftovers from World War II. The nonsmokers would trade their cigarettes for whatever extra food they could make deals for. One of the more common ways to make some of the less desirable meals taste better was to cook up our not-so-famous steel-pot-stew. After removing the inside leather liners, we could use our steel helmets like a pot. We put in different food combinations along with whatever spices we had, which almost also included a heavy dose of Tabasco sauce, and heated it up over a heat tablet or a small piece of plastic explosive. It was a far cry from gourmet but sometimes we would actually wind up with a fairly tasty meal. The helmets were pretty versatile. In addition to protecting our heads and substituting as cooking pots, we used them to hold water for shaving. And who knows, maybe that actually contributed to the improved flavor of the food we cooked in them.

When we went into the field on our recon missions, we had to travel as light as possible, so instead of C-Rats we often took LRRP (Long Range Recon Patrol) rations. The *lerp* rations, as we called them, consisted of freeze-dried meals in sealed plastic bags. They were the predecessors to MREs (Meals Ready to Eat) used by the military today. We simply tore open the bag, added water, and stirred. And any time we were able to heat the water we had an instant hot meal. To me, they were like gourmet meals, much better than even the best tasting C-Rats. Chicken and Rice was my all-time favorite. We had heat tablets that could be used to heat water, coffee or soup, but they took much too long to get the liquid hot. The better alternative was to use a small piece of C-4, which is a plastic explosive. It takes a firing cap to make it explode, but lighting it with a flame from a match or lighter just causes it to burn extremely hot. A very small piece under a C-ration can would get the liquid inside piping hot in seconds.

Most of the other operational and support personnel were housed in separate reinforced and sandbag covered bunkers, which of course had electricity. The TOC (Tactical Operations Center) was where the officers would work on their tactical strategies and plans. It came as quite a shock to our company commander when someone discovered the company TOC had been built next to a live bomb buried just a few feet in the ground. It was a 500-pound bomb that had been dropped on suspected enemy positions long before the hilltop was turned into a fire base. The captain didn't waste time getting it quickly, but very carefully, dug out and removed. A Shit-Hook (slang for a CH-47 Chinook helicopter) came in and carried it away. The fire base also was home to an artillery battery, as were virtually all the firebases in the Cav's AO (Area of Operation). Our artillery support unit consisted of six 105mm Howitzer guns which were called on regularly to support the guys in the field. The first few times I was on the base when those guns fired I could feel the ground vibrate and the noise was deafening. But after a while it simply became a part of everyday life, in the same way I got accustomed to living with the weather and the bugs.

Chapter 10 – Guerilla Warfare

The challenges we faced in Vietnam were very different from those of previous wars. In those earlier conflicts there were well-defined lines of battle, normally with U.S. and allied forces on one side and enemy forces on the other. In Vietnam, however, there were no defined battle lines. The entire country was the battle field. In previous wars we knew who the enemy was, readily recognizable regular soldiers from the country we were battling. In Vietnam we were not only fighting the regular NVA (North Vietnam Army) soldiers, we were also fighting the VC (Viet Cong), who were the South Vietnamese guerillas fighting to help reunify North and South Vietnam under communist rule. The NVA soldiers were usually identifiable by their regular army fatigues and tan or green pith helmets. The VC, on the other hand, normally wore traditional Vietnamese clothing consisting of black pajamas, straw coolie hats, and rubber sandals, making it impossible to distinguish the good guys from the bad guys, unless they were carrying weapons. The Russian AK-47 automatic assault rifle was the weapon of choice for both the NVA and VC. It was a safe bet that any Vietnamese spotted carrying one of those rifles was a VC, and hopefully he would soon be a dead VC.

I could never understand why the majority of our base camps hired so many Vietnamese civilians from nearby villages to work in the compounds. There's no doubt that some of those workers who portrayed themselves as friendly civilians were in fact VC themselves. They acted like our friends during the day, but were our deadly enemies at night. And others, maybe not actual VC themselves, were sympathizers who passed strategic information about our camps to their comrades, often resulting in U.S. casualties. One example of this was when a rocket attack made multiple direct hits on our ammo dump, which just a few days earlier had been moved from one area of the base to another. Those rockets could not have struck with such accuracy if the exact coordinates of the new location had not been known in advance. And obviously they were, thanks to their comrades working as our friends.

Many times, patrols would go through what was supposed to be a friendly village, only to be fired on by hidden VC. They would be waiting in tunnels for our guys to pass through, fire at them as they were leaving the village, and then vanish into their tunnels or the woods. That happened often enough that villages where there were signs of a trap or ambush would first be checked by doing a *recon by fire*—fire into the suspected enemy locations before they had a chance to spring their ambush. It is unfortunate when noncombatants become casualties, but it's virtually impossible not to have some *collateral damage* in any war, and especially when the enemy uses guerilla tactics and civilians as shields. What's more, when you are in a war zone and your survival is at stake, you take whatever actions are necessary to keep yourself and your fellow soldiers alive.

In addition to the monsoon rains, the sweltering heat, and the oppressive humidity, the Vietnam landscape itself presented challenges that American forces were unaccustomed to. We were faced with jungles unbelievably thick with trees and heavy undergrowth, and canopies that blocked almost all sunlight and often prevented artillery shells from penetrating their dense layers. There was razor sharp elephant grass that often grew well in excess of six feet tall, rice paddies that had to be crossed with no ground cover available, and trails that were booby-trapped with punji pits and a wide variety of explosive devices. A punji pit is a camouflaged hole in the trail with pointed wooden stakes sticking up from the bottom. The stakes are normally smeared either with poison or human or animal feces. The hole could be just a little larger than a human foot or large enough for a person to fall into. The enemy's hope was that the poison would kill if the stakes didn't. And much of the area was full of underground tunnels and caverns, which the enemy used for everything from simple hiding places to elaborate complexes for ammunition and weapons, general supply storage, living quarters, and even well-equipped medical clinics.

Any time we found one of the tunnels our standing order was to have one of our men check it out. That meant someone crawling in with only a pistol and a flashlight, hoping like crazy the tunnel was empty. If there was a VC waiting with a loaded AK-47, whoever entered wouldn't stand a chance. And even if the tunnel was empty there was always the possibility that it was booby-trapped. Those who went into the tunnels regularly were called *tunnel rats.* We didn't have a regular tunnel rat in my unit, and only one guy of our guys was small enough to get into the tunnels. He wasn't on every mission, so we were not always able to physically check every tunnel we found. But whether we were able to or not, the first thing we always did was toss a smoke grenade inside. That was followed by regular grenades, not only into that same hole, but also into any exit or vent holes that we could see smoke escaping from. On a few occasions we found sizable weapon caches, including grenades, AK-47's, machine guns, mortar tubes, rocket launchers and quite a large amount of ammunition.

The jungles were also full of natural predators—snakes, scorpions, fire ants, leeches, and even an occasional tiger. Many of the snakes were harmless but others were extremely poisonous and very deadly, like the Bamboo Viper or Chinese Green-Tree Viper. That's the one we referred to as the *Two-Step Snake or Mister Two-Step*. Luckily I never saw one, but apparently a single bite would leave its victim dead before he could take two steps. We often had to wade across streams and creeks, even cross rivers, and no matter what we did to prevent it, more often than not we would be covered with leeches by the time we reached the other side. Tying our pants tight around our ankles would help a little, but that didn't stop some of them from getting onto the skin, and sometimes into the worst of body places. If we tried pulling them off, their heads would break off and stay buried in the skin, which often resulted in serious infections. The only way to safely remove the leeches was to spray them with insect repellent or touch them with a flame or the end of a lit cigarette, but even then there was always the possibility of infection.

Scorpions, trying to stay cool during the day, would hide behind small stones and twigs, and fire ants frequently made their homes at the base of trees. Wherever we sat when taking a break in the field, there would be a good possibility of disturbing them and suffering the consequences. Fire ants are a far cry from typical picnic ants. It's hard to describe what it's like being attacked by hundreds of giant red ants with big pincers and blister-producing stingers—let me just say it's not the ideal way to get out of the field.

Also different from other wars was the amount of time we spent in actual combat. During World War II infantrymen averaged 40 days in combat over a four-year period. That's an average of *ten days a year*. I don't mean to imply that World War II soldiers had it easy, because they certainly did not. Some of the battles they fought may have been relatively short but were as brutal as any in recent history, and more so than most. But in Vietnam the average number of days a grunt (infantryman) spent in combat in a one-year period was *two-hundred and forty*. And even my small recon unit was no exception. While our primary mission was to gather information about enemy strengths and movements *without making contact*, that was only on paper. In reality, we were involved in enemy contact almost every time we left our base. Often those contacts resulted from Charlie walking into our ambushes, but there were instances when we were the ones ambushed, and other times when we just happened to run into an enemy patrol. And in spite of the number of times we had contact with the enemy, we sustained very few casualties.

That's quite ironic when you consider how Echo Company was formed. It was with men from other companies in the division whose commanding officers felt were not good enough combat soldiers to hang on to. How wrong those commanders were! Their castoffs were warriors of the highest caliber. In Echo Company's first year of operation we had the highest kill ratio of any unit in the First Cavalry Division during that same time period. We did suffer casualties, but we were fortunate to have had only a few deaths during my time with the company. (In the Addendum section of the book there is a copy of an article published in the Cavalair Magazine about Echo Recon's early history).

A few times, after being out in the boonies for days at a time, we would get a break from the field. Once we even got to spend a day at a nearby beach on the South China Sea. I don't know if it had an official name but we called it Wonder Beach, maybe because we were able to totally forget the war, even for just a few hours. It felt almost like being at a beach in the States, except no other people were around, and no boardwalk or fast food joints—just a bunch of grunts splashing each other in the water. Most of the time, however, a break from the field resulted in pulling base guard duty. Officers and specialized personnel, such as medics, were not normally involved, but the rest of us were assigned to defensive bunkers or other security positions around the base. As a squad leader, I only stood guard duty once in awhile.

Aside from Wonder Beach and the occasional days spent at the base camp, I once managed to get a two-day break from the field. One day after the division moved south to Tay Ninh, I was given permission to go to finance to get a payroll problem straightened out. Most of our division support hadn't yet moved south which meant I had to go back to An Khe. I wasn't able to get there direct on that day so I first caught a hop to Phu Cat Air Force Base, about 25 miles east of An Khe, and stayed there overnight. The Air Force ran missions around the clock from Phu Cat so they maintained a twenty-four-hour mess hall. That was where I had an absolutely wonderful steak dinner, just the way I liked it—medium rare and smothered in onions. It was the best meal I had during my entire time in 'Nam, even better than many steaks I had eaten in the States. And I got to sleep in a real bed in an air-conditioned barracks. I was amazed at how different life there was compared to the base I had just left. There were wooden sidewalks, air-conditioned buildings, a big PX, even NCO and Officer Clubs. It felt like I was on a military base in the States, especially the way everyone was dressed. All the men I saw were wearing starched fatigues and spit-shined shoes, had short haircuts, were clean shaven, and were unarmed. No one except the Military Police carried weapons. I had to leave my M-16 behind, but the .45 strapped to my thigh, coupled with my ragged clothes and shabby look, got me a lot of stares from the base personnel. It was as though they didn't know there was a war going on. The whole thing made me very uncomfortable, but I did enjoy the food, the bed, and the break from the field. I got to the finance office in An Khe the next morning, was back in Phu Cat later that afternoon, stayed overnight again, and got back to my unit the following afternoon. And of course my financial issue never did get resolved until well after I was out of the army.

The times I was out of the field while with Echo Company were a pleasant break from direct combat, but even then the threat of incoming rockets and the possibility of the base getting overrun were always on my mind. I'm sure the men stationed at Phu Cat and other large bases thought they were in pretty safe places, and compared to being in the boonies or on Fire Bases in the middle of the jungle, they definitely were. But even those bases were never totally safe from enemy mortars and rockets. One of our men got transferred to a rear base as an officer's jeep driver and was thrilled to be out of the field. It wasn't more than a week or so after his transfer that the base he was on was attacked and his jeep took a direct hit from an enemy mortar round, killing him instantly. He was the only one in the jeep at the time and the only death during that attack.

Chapter 11 - Combat

As good as my training was in NCO School, I knew I wasn't fully prepared for the real thing. Even though I was put in charge of a squad, my lack of actual combat experience left me with some uncertainty about my ability to make sound decisions under live-fire conditions. All the guys in my squad had been on at least a few patrols or ambushes before I arrived, so they had already been exposed to things I had yet to experience. I was the *FNG,* and they could not possibly have any confidence in me until I proved myself to them. So before my first mission I got my squad together and told them how much I would be counting on them to keep me from screwing up. I didn't want to do anything that might get someone hurt or killed, so I wanted their help and advice until I felt comfortable enough to lead the squad on my own. It was a good move and it went a long way toward earning the trust and respect of my men, while I gained confidence in myself.

It didn't upset me in the least that my first few missions were uneventful. The first one was a two-squad recon sweep close to the base, with the other squad leading the patrol. The next mission was similar, but that time my squad took the point and again it was without incident. There was no contact and I was perfectly fine with that. The next two missions were single-squad ambushes, the first one at night, the second during the day, and I relied on my men to help me get them set up properly. Nothing happened on the first one, but the next one became my trial under fire. Shortly after we set up close to an intersection of two small trails we spotted five gooks coming our way. Actually we heard them before we saw them. They apparently gave no thought to the possibility of being ambushed because they were talking and laughing as they casually strolled down the trail. A few of them even had their rifles carelessly slung over their shoulders. When they got into the intersection we set off our claymore mines and opened fire, getting very little return fire back. They were caught completely off guard and it was over in less than a minute. Three were killed, the other two somehow managed to crawl away into the woods. We suffered no casualties, and I had survived my first firefight. After the dust settled, so to speak, we searched the bodies for any useful intelligence and then moved them off the trail. Dead bodies in war movies can be made to look extremely gory, but it's nothing compared to real life, especially when they're riddled with bullet holes. Blood was everywhere— even pieces of brains and guts were visible. One of the dead bodies had shattered bones sticking out of a leg, all three had multiple holes in the stomach and chest, and one had been also been shot in the head. The looked like kids, maybe all of 16 years old. It was a gruesome sight, and it took a real effort to keep from puking. I drank some water, caught my breath, and mumbled to the RTO to call in a contact report and a KIA (Killed in Action) body count.

Shooting at people who shoot back is a far cry from firing at stationary cardboard targets, and I readily admit I was scared shitless. And the thought that I probably killed one or more of them wasn't an easy thing for me to deal with. All the way back to the base I kept reliving the incident in my mind. From my vantage point I couldn't see exactly where my bullets hit, so there was no way to tell for sure if they hit any of them. It all happened so fast it made me dizzy. I didn't want to believe I killed another human being, but I had to force myself to accept the fact that it was most likely I did. And even if not that time, I knew another firefight would surely result in the inevitable. Maybe it wouldn't be tomorrow or the next day, but it would happen. I pictured myself facing a VC, my rifle on full automatic, my finger holding down the trigger, watching my bullets tear him apart. It wasn't a pleasant thought, but it was painfully obvious that if I wanted to get home in one piece to my wife and daughter, that's exactly what I would have to do. I wouldn't have a choice. It's a pretty callous way of thinking but that's what it takes to survive in war—do unto them before they have a chance to do it unto you. After a while it was less and less bothersome; pulling the trigger was easier, and killing gooks became almost as normal as going to a civilian job every day. I know that sounds insane, but no one ever said war is rational.

On a recon mission not long after joining Echo Recon my squad was on a narrow trail when our point man spotted a single VC slowly coming toward us on a cross trail. The point man stopped and ducked down, as did the rest of us, and when the gook was just a few yards away he shot him with a short automatic burst from his M-16. After waiting a few minutes to make sure the dead gook had been alone, the point man did a quick search of the body, then literally picked it up and tossed it off the trail into the bushes. It was as though it was a bag of trash and he was simply throwing it away. There were no signs of remorse or emotion whatsoever. To him, and everyone else in the squad, it was simply another dead gook, one less able to kill Americans. And after the incident was radioed in to our rear command we continued on our mission as though nothing had happened—just another routine day in the boonies.

As part of our standard ambush procedures we placed Claymore mines pointed outward from our position toward the trail we were hoping Charlie would come down. The M-18 Claymore mine is a directional, command-detonated anti-personnel mine, meaning it is activated by remote-control. The device has a pair of legs that are pushed into the ground, and when triggered, it sends a wide pattern of metal balls into the kill zone like a shotgun. The detonator is a hand plunger that's attached by wire to the Claymore itself. On one of our night ambushes we set up a semi-circle perimeter, surrounded by Claymores and trip flares. During the night we heard noises all around us, but the flares were never set off, and we never saw any movement on the trail, in the bushes, or in the trees behind us. Even though we never heard voices and assumed the noises were being made by animals, every man was wide awake and stayed alert all night, with rifles ready and hands on the Claymore plungers, ready to detonate.

Fortunately, we never set off any of the Claymores, and in the morning we realized just how lucky we were. If we had set them off we all could have been killed or seriously wounded. The noises we heard obviously were made by Charlie, hoping we would set off our Claymores because they had managed to sneak up to them and turn them around to face us, without our knowing it. When we realized what happened we were all visibly shaken by how close we came to being blown to bits. Following that incident we purposely booby-trapped each of the Claymores to prevent the same thing from happening again. Any attempt to pull them out of the ground would activate a hidden pressure switch that would trigger the Claymore. If we had no contact, we would deactivate the pressure switches before removing the mines.

During the six months I was with Echo Recon we had a lot of enemy contact and did suffer a number of casualties, but we were fortunate to have only three fatalities during that time. Were there forces at work that kept those numbers low or were we just plain lucky? Why didn't we set off the Claymores when we heard noises? Why does one man walk away from a firefight unscathed while the two guys practically shoulder to shoulder on either side of him get wounded or killed? Why them and not the guy in the middle? Could he have done something to save his buddies? Why does nothing happen to one man who picks up something off the ground as a souvenir, while someone else does the very same thing and loses an arm or his life to a booby-trap? Why does one man get sick minutes before going out on a mission and the helicopter he would have been on crashes, killing all those on board? Why does one man walk away unscathed while others aren't as fortunate? Is it destiny, luck, or just coincidence? I know these are questions with no answers, yet that that doesn't stop me from thinking about them, or the survivor guilt that eventually followed.

On one platoon-size ambush we got into a pretty heavy firefight, and our platoon leader called for artillery support. He gave the coordinates to the artillery unit back at the base and requested one round to be fired for accuracy—a common practice. Either the lieutenant screwed up the coordinates or one of the artillery men did, because the round fell extremely short. So short, in fact, that it landed right in the middle of our position. Miraculously, it did not explode. It happened so fast, I didn't realize what was happening. I heard its whistling sound getting louder as it approached, but instead of continuing past our position, the whistling was replaced with a whoosh, flowed by a loud thud. The artillery shell had burrowed into the ground close enough to five or six of us that we could reach out and touch it. If it had exploded, there's no doubt we would have been statistics. But it was a dud, defective in some way, which prevented it from detonating. Even though the lieutenant called in a new set of coordinates, which were right on target, the gooks had apparently taken off when they heard that first shell coming in. All we found when we searched the area were holes in the ground. And although no one was hurt from that incident, it still brought on the most recurring unanswerable question of all: *why am I still alive?*

A similar short round incident occurred when an artillery shell hit and exploded in the trees directly above our position. We were directly below the explosive rain of shrapnel, yet not a single man was struck. Was it a miraculous incident, divine intervention, or just plain luck? As our circumstances didn't give us the luxury of deep philosophical discussions, we just considered ourselves damned lucky and moved on. But those thoughts of *how* and *why* would creep back into my consciousness, and I'm quite sure it was the same for many other guys as well. Sadly, *friendly fire* accidents happened all too often. And they have occurred in virtually every conflict before and after Vietnam. It's bad enough when casualties are caused by the enemy, but it's many times worse for those affected when they result from the actions of their own forces. It's one of the hazards of war that no one has control over, no matter what kind of precautions are taken or how good everyone does their job. It just happens.

A few other friendly fire incidents that I was involved in did result in casualties, but fortunately no deaths. One such occurrence was when two of our Cobra helicopter gunships fired rockets at us. It was a two squad recon mission and we were walking down a trail on one side of a long ridge. Unknown to us, a column of NVA soldiers was going down the other side of the same ridge, and as a Huey (Bell UH-1 helicopter) flew over the ridge the gooks fired at it. Although the door gunners could easily have returned fire, the chopper pilot immediately took evasive action and flew out of range of the incoming stream of bullets. As it turned away from the ridge, two Cobra gunships (Bell AH-1 Cobra Helicopters) that had been hiding inside nearby clouds flew in to attack the enemy. The gooks stopped firing and got out of sight the moment they saw the Cobras jump out of their cloud cover. We saw the gunships heading in our direction, thinking they had their sights on the other side of the ridge. But the only movement the lead gunship pilot saw was us, and before we had a chance to let him know we were friendly troops, the Cobra came swooping down the trail we were on and let loose with its rockets. There was immediate chaos with everyone trying to get off the trail and behind trees. Our RTO popped smoke (threw out smoke grenades to mark our position) and tried making radio contact with our rear command. But the second gunship also fired rockets before they realized we were the good guys. As the rocket barrages hit, shrapnel flew in all directions, concussions from the blasts literally blew us off our feet, and almost everyone got hit.

All of the men were wearing soft *boonie* hats, except one guy. He was wearing his steel helmet, which he rarely did. A pretty good sized piece of shrapnel hit the his helmet dead center above his eyebrows, but it didn't penetrate the metal. All he wound up with was a minor concussion and a bad headache; there was no doubt the helmet saved his life. I had a very small piece of shrapnel in my left forearm that just barely broke the skin. Our medic was busy patching up guys with much more serious wounds so I just pulled it out myself and stuck a band-aid on the tiny cut. Since the medic never saw the piece of shrapnel in my arm, he said he couldn't put me in for a Purple Heart. That was fine with me. I was happy as hell just to be alive.

Fighting for your life day after day, seeing the results of extreme torture and brutalization of your fellow soldiers, and witnessing the death and disfigurement of innocent men, women, and children, can bring out retaliatory vindictiveness and cruelty in individuals that never would have occurred under any other circumstances. It is often said that war turns boys into men, but in some cases it turns those same boys into wild animals who are unable to control the brutality of their actions. When American soldiers are discovered having been horribly mutilated or tied to trees with their own body parts sticking out of their mouths, or when bodies of fellow soldiers are found booby-trapped in an attempt to kill or maim more Americans, it should not be surprising that such sights can unleash a desire to inflict similar atrocities against the perpetrators. Patrols have gotten ambushed resulting in one of the men getting trapped in a no-mans-land between our men and the enemy, and the gooks would just keep shooting him. They were not trying to kill him, they wanted to inflict more pain and suffering in the hope his buddies would try to rescue him and become targets themselves. If you are faced with that situation and don't try to help, you're forced to watch helplessly as a brother GI is subjected to a slow, torturous death. If you do try to help, you could easily end up taking that guy's place. It's a no-win situation. The only logical compassionate way out is to put your fellow warrior out of his misery, but that's something most of us could not and would not do. So you do nothing, and relive the despair of your inaction in haunting nightmares and flashbacks, and suffer the agonizing pain of survivor guilt for the rest of your life.

The VC and NVA committed many atrocities against civilian villagers simply because they supported the South Vietnam government and were friendly to U. S. soldiers. Men, women, and children of all ages were maimed and killed, village leaders were tortured and executed in front of their villagers, women were raped, and pregnant women had their unborn babies literally cut out of their bodies and butchered before their eyes. And these are just a few of the horrors too many of our soldiers were exposed to over and over again. Yet despite the anger and desire for revenge, there were very few acts of retribution even though many in the media reported otherwise.

Yes, there were incidents such as the Mei Lai massacre, and ears of dead VC were cut off and strung together to make souvenir necklaces. Unlike video war games, actual war can turn sane, rational people into cruel, brutal, out-of-control killers. When civilized human beings are battling one another to the death, they can lose all sense of humanity and revert to basic animal instincts. It's survival of the fittest to the extreme. But those acts of retribution were clearly the exceptions. And while I certainly do not condone them, I understand where they came from. And I can say with all honesty that during my time with Echo Recon we never engaged in retaliatory atrocities of any sort. Yes, we killed our share of gooks. And yes, purposely killing another human being for any reason, and by any means, can be looked upon as an atrocity. But in war it's necessary to use whatever means are available to kill the enemy. And not just with grenades and small arms fire, but also artillery, mortars, rockets, bombs, even flame-throwers and napalm. It's that or be killed yourself.

When you get shot at from a hut in a village you don't have the luxury of checking for innocent civilians inside before returning fire. And if there are VC in there using women and children as shields unbeknownst to you is it your fault that those innocent civilians get wounded or killed as a result? What about when a ten or twelve-year-old boy comes running up to your passing patrol trying to sell you a bottle of coca cola, but you think he has a live grenade in his hand ready to throw at you? It looks like a grenade and you know from experience that innocent-looking Vietnamese kids were known to toss grenades at American soldiers. Do you shoot him? If you don't and it's a live grenade, it's too late to react when it's thrown at your patrol. You and maybe some of your buddies are dead. And if you do shoot him and see that it was actually a soda bottle in his hand, then what? You had to make a split-second decision, a decision with your life and the lives of your comrades in the balance, so you squeeze the trigger and then see the soda bottle drop from his hand as he falls to the ground. A young boy dies at your hands and you have to live with that forever. It's regrettable when innocent civilians become casualties of war simply because they happened to be in the wrong place at the wrong time. It's a rotten consequence of war, but I'm not aware of anyone who has devised a way to fight a *civilized* war—a war in which only the soldiers get hurt. Maybe that's only possible in video games and movies.

When soldiers are exposed to events of this sort on a regular basis one of two things could happen. Some might develop what is referred to in the medical community as *combat stress reaction*, while others usually become emotionally numb to the death and devastation they see and participate in. Combat stress reaction is when a soldier gets to the point of not being able to function effectively as a consequence of repetitive exposure to traumatic experiences, and has to be removed from the battlefield. In previous wars these men were said to have *battle fatigue* or they suffered from *shell-shock*. Shell-shock was used to describe reactions to the intensity of the bombardment and fighting that produced a helplessness appearing as panic or flight, or an inability to reason, sleep, walk or even talk. Thanks to the body's built-in safety mechanisms, most combat soldiers do not develop combat stress, at least not while still in the war zone, and not with noticeable symptoms. To prevent combat stress, the mind is able to stop emotional responses to trauma from affecting the soldier's ability to function effectively. This is accomplished by immobilizing the emotional system, completely shutting it down, resulting in total emotional numbness.

Chapter 12 – Luck or Fate

Some guys died on their first day in Vietnam, while others died just days, even hours, before they were scheduled to leave the country. Most of our casualties happened in the field, but rocket and mortar attacks on supposedly safe bases took many lives as well. There were no real safe areas in Vietnam, which kept my fear and anxiety levels pretty high. It was there whether I was in the field, on a chopper, on the base between missions, even the few times I got to one of those so-called *safe* bases. During a firefight, however, adrenaline takes over, leaving no time to think about fear, you just focus on keeping yourself and your buddies alive. The fear is still there, but its something you adapt to—it's there but it doesn't prevent you from doing what you have to do.

And a certain amount of fear isn't a bad thing. Actually, it can be a key factor in keeping you alert and vigilant, and that just might help you stay alive. Letting your guard down a little bit, even for an instant, can be disastrous for you and your fellow soldiers. Not being observant on patrol can result in triggering a booby trap or walking into an ambush, and not being alert and wide awake when it's your turn on night watch can open the door for Charlie to overrun your position. That's one of the reasons I hardly ever slept when we were out at night, even though we took turns being on watch—half on, half off. I was always afraid one of the guys who was supposed to be awake might fall asleep, so I didn't. I'd wait until we were back on base and then try to grab some sleep whenever I could.

Some of the guys maintained they were never scared, not even once during their entire time there. I could understand that if it came from guys who spent all their time in rear areas, but, in my opinion, those who were in combat and say they were never scared are full of crap. They're either knowingly lying or have repeated it so many times they've talked themselves into believing it. Either way, I think it's impossible not to experience some amount of fear in the face of imminent life threatening danger. And it's certainly nothing to be ashamed of. John Wayne may have said it best: *"Courage is being scared to death... and saddling up anyway."*

On the opposite side of that issue are those soldiers who are unable to handle the fear, no matter how hard they try. In my unit there were a few guys who were so terrified during firefights they became incapable of functioning. Not only couldn't they fire their rifles, they couldn't stop shaking and were hardly able to talk. It would have been foolish to even think about sending them back into the boonies in that emotional state. Not only would their lives have been at risk, their inaction could have jeopardized the lives of everyone on the mission. The safest thing was to transfer them to some type of non-combat duty, which is what was normally done. And of course we also had a few guys who wanted to be out of the field so badly they would do almost anything to make it happen. It wasn't a question of not be able to handle it, they just wanted out. Some men would constantly complain to the medics about non-existent ailments—headaches, backaches, stomach aches, anything at all—hoping to get put on a light-duty medical profile that would get them out of the field, even for just a short time. And then there were those who purposely injured themselves to keep from going on missions. We had one guy who said his rifle accidentally discharged, shooting himself in the foot. And not just once, it happened twice. On his first try, the bullet somehow missed his toes and all he got out of it was a hole in his boot. The second time he was more successful, he blew off one of his toes and got his wish, a medevac ride to the hospital. He didn't come back during the remainder of my time with Echo Recon, and after that I don't know if he made it back or not. And, as I already mentioned, there were guys who would stick an arm or leg out of their bunkers during a mortar or rocket attack, hoping for a magic bullet to send them home.

During one recon patrol we stopped around mid-afternoon for a short break. Our point man was sitting on a small rock cleaning his .45 when we heard a shot ring out, followed by loud cursing and a yell of pain. Moochie, which is what we called him, had gunshot wounds in both his hand and leg. At first we all thought he must have done it to himself, either accidentally or on purpose, like the guy who shot himself in the foot. But both of those possibilities were quickly dismissed as the sniper who shot him fired again from the tree he was hiding in. Fortunately he missed on his second shot and no one else was hit. Moochie's wounds were not life threatening, they just looked much worse than they actually were, even though I'm sure they were pretty painful. We returned fire into the tree but the sniper immediately took off and vanished into the jungle. We called in a medevac chopper and Moochie was flown to the closest field hospital. After getting a temporary patch job, he was sent to a rear hospital until his wounds were fully healed, and it wasn't long before he returned, back walking point.

A few months after I came to Echo Company we got a new platoon leader, a second lieutenant fresh out of OCS. He had no combat experience but thought he knew everything there was to know about commanding an infantry platoon. In spite of how great a platoon leader he thought he was his poor judgment and unwillingness to accept sound advice resulted in serious casualties. We were on a recon mission when we spotted a small squad of NVA soldiers coming down a hill, heading right toward us. We quickly set up an improvised ambush, and as soon as they got into the open area at the bottom of the hill our machine gunner opened up on them with his M-60, and the rest of us fired at them as well. It was over in seconds; two gooks were dead and the others managed to escape into the woods, even though we were sure a few of them had been wounded. I don't think any of them even got a shot off. When the fighting stopped, the lieutenant ordered two men to check the dead soldiers' bodies for any useful intelligence information that might be on them. His concern for the men was overshadowed by his desire to return to base with something that might make him look good to our company commander. We, the squad leaders and platoon sergeant, tried to convince him that he was making a big mistake. The bodies were lying out in the open and we had no way to know if any of the other gooks were still around. If they were, anyone approaching those bodies would be easy targets, but he wouldn't listen to us. The two men he selected were searching the bodies when they were fired at from a gook that had been hiding behind a tree, seriously wounding them both. As we returned fire, more gooks began shooting at us, hitting our platoon sergeant in the center of his forehead. Staff Sergeant Curtis Oren Smith, Jr. was a career soldier who had transferred from a line company to Echo Company just a few weeks earlier. He was on his second tour. He was dead before his body hit the ground. I'm not sure exactly how the incident was reported to our captain but the lieutenant never went on any missions with us again, and we had a new platoon leader soon after. Had he been allowed to remain with us, there's no doubt that his poor judgment and reckless decisions would have continued to put our men in danger. That is unless he happened to get himself killed first. The last I heard he was transferred to a rear unit, fortunately for everyone.

Unfortunately, episodes like that one were much too common in Vietnam. Second Lieutenants with little or no combat experience, who would take no advice from their war-seasoned sergeants, were a constant danger to their own men. They were delusional, thinking their high marks in OCS and a silver bar on their collar meant they knew what to do in combat situations. They apparently believed that gave them the know-how to do the same in the middle of a real firefight. They were assholes who regularly put the lives of their men in jeopardy.

Then, too, there were experienced officers who cared more about getting medals and advancing their careers than they did about the men who became casualties because of those ambitions. They were men seemingly unaffected by the deaths they caused. To them, casualties were simply a by-product of war, even if they were their own men, killed as a result of their irresponsible decisions. They looked at it as the nature of the beast, the nature of war. I don't have first-hand knowledge myself, but there are many stories of *fragging* incidents during the Vietnam War. That's when an officer, whose men believed their lives were put in unnecessary danger because of his stupid decisions, was shot or killed from a grenade thrown by one of his own men.

There were times when we just happened to come across dead bodies, or what was left of them after they had become meals for the maggots and vultures. Sometimes we would find them deep in the woods and other times lying right in the middle of the trail we were on. Often they were VC, probably killed by artillery or machine guns from helicopter door gunners. There were also times we found shallow graves, some with just a single body in them and others with more bodies than we wanted to count. The smell of a dead body is like nothing else I can relate to. I thought burning shit was bad, but that's mild compared to a corpse that's been rotting in the ground for days, weeks or even months. The longer it's been in the ground the more intense and sickening it is. I can't put it into words, but it is something I will never forget. The first time I saw the flies, worms, and maggots covering a dead body, eating away at the flesh, it was impossible to keep from puking. Yet, as horrible as that was, it didn't take long to get used to such sights. Again, we adapt as a matter of survival, even to the deadly horrors of war.

Many of the incidents I was involved in have caused me many sleepless nights ever since I left the service. But there were three in particular that still haunt me regularly. Two were with Echo Recon, and the third was after I was transferred to the Brigade Civil Affairs unit. Earlier I mentioned the death of our platoon sergeant, Staff Sergeant Smith, from a bullet to the head. While we had been arguing with the lieutenant about checking the dead body, additional NVA of platoon-size or larger reinforced the small squad we had ambushed. And that's who we were in the firefight with when the sergeant got shot. During the firefight we sustained additional wounded and called for medevacs to get the casualties out. Because of constant enemy fire the choppers couldn't land in the nearby clearing, and with no other open space, the pilots had to hover above the trees behind us—dropping harnesses down to hoist up the wounded. In spite of artillery shells pounding their positions, the gooks were able to keep the choppers at bay with intense ground fire for quite some time. Even after we were able to get some of the wounded out the enemy gunfire never completely stopped. The final medevac chopper had just hoisted the last of the wounded aboard and was in the process of doing the same with Sergeant Smith's body. A harness was strapped across his mid-section and under his arms, and his chin bounced against his chest as he was pulled up. The body was part way up, but not clear of the trees, when the chopper began taking on much heavier enemy fire. To avoid getting shot down, the pilot had no choice but to get out of range, and do it fast. And that's exactly what he did, with the sergeant's swinging body banging into one tree after another as the chopper flew off. As gruesome as it was to watch the body banging into the trees, it was as if I was mesmerized in some kind of hypnotic trance. Even though enemy bullets were also being fired in my direction, I was unable to turn my head away until the chopper was completely out of sight. And almost every time I hear the unique whomp-whomp sounds of a Huey overhead, my mind replays that scenario like a slow-motion movie. When I hear those first distinctive sounds I know what's coming, yet I am usually unable to stop it from happening.

One of my most terrifying and mystifying events, however, was a face-to-face encounter with an NVA point man that could have easily blown me away, but for some unknown reason didn't. I was staring at certain death, expecting a bullet to come at me in less time than I could blink, yet no bullet came, and I walked away unharmed. Even though we had a few guys who were exceptionally good point men and often volunteered for it, I felt I should not assign my men to do anything I wouldn't do myself. So on one of our platoon-size recon missions I decided it was time for me to be the point man. It was an early December morning, my squad was leading the patrol and I was on point. We had been flown by chopper to a spot about ten klicks (a klick is one kilometer, just over six-tenths of a mile) from our base camp. We had to jump off the helicopters into some pretty thick elephant grass but made it into the woods without incident. We walked along a trail thick with branches, vines, and underbrush, which limited visibility considerably. I was about 10 yards ahead of the rest of my squad when the trail took a slight curve to the right. As I cautiously followed it around, I was suddenly facing a young NVA soldier who had just turned onto my trail from a smaller cross trail. We could not have been more than 20 feet from each other. My rifle was on full automatic and the safety was off, but the barrel was pointed slightly downward. If I fired, the best I could have hoped for was to hit him in the legs. His AK-47 was pointing directly at my chest, so firing without raising my rifle would have meant instant death for me. And if I raised my rifle I knew he could shoot me before I could get him, so I just froze. The closest man behind me saw that I had stopped, but because of the curve in the trail he couldn't see why, so he stopped and motioned for the guys behind him to do the same. The NVA soldier and I stared at each other for what seemed like an eternity but was actually no more than a second or two. Then, as he lowered his rifle, he turned back to the trail he had turned off of, and just continued on that trail. I immediately ducked down into the brush and counted about a dozen NVA soldiers as they followed their point man and walked right past my trail. I stayed hidden in the bushes for a while after they passed just to be sure there weren't any others lagging behind. As soon as I was certain they were all well past me, I moved back to our platoon leader's position and reported the NVA movement, but without mentioning my encounter with the enemy point man.

I can only guess that the NVA soldier must have reported seeing an American patrol to his superior, and if he did so, he probably omitted our face-to-face encounter as well. I had one of my guys take over the point, and we slowly followed the trail they were on for the better part of the morning. The NVA patrol may have guessed we were going to follow them or may have heard our movement behind them. Either way, an ambush was waiting for us, which we walked right into. Apparently the group we were tracking met up with a larger force, and it was their trap that we walked into. Even though we were able to get artillery support, they kept us pinned down with machine gun and mortar fire well into the night. Somewhere around 3:00 a.m. an enemy mortar shell exploded in the trees directly above our position, dropping shrapnel into the entire area. This time we weren't lucky. We had 15 wounded, 12 of which were pretty serious, and one guy was killed. He had been directly under the exploding mortar and his body was completely riddled with shrapnel.

When daylight came, we managed to move back to a reasonably safe area and set up a landing zone for medevac and pickup choppers. By that time, we were short on ammunition, had almost no food left, and the wounded included our platoon sergeant and platoon leader. The medevacs came in first to take out the casualties and our company commander came in with them. He was a West Point graduate and a very gung-ho Ranger before taking command of Echo Company. His first action was to appoint me temporary platoon sergeant and then he ordered me to get the remaining men prepared to go after the gooks who just kicked our asses.

I understood his wanting to go after them because I felt the same, but I thought he was being unrealistic under the circumstances. We had lost half our men, the rest of us were pretty beat up, and we were extremely low on ammo. And he wanted us to go after them immediately, without waiting for reinforcements or additional supplies. In spite of his combat experience, I felt he was making an emotional decision instead of a sound strategic one. It was an order I could not carry out. I wasn't about to let the men go on a mission I believed would result in almost certain suicide. I respectfully told him I would get the men ready, but only for a return to our base camp, not to walk into another disaster. I just stood there while he insisted we would return to base only after we first took care of the gooks. It was a direct order, and if I refused again he would have me up for a court-martial. Hearing that, I casually rested my hand on the handle of my .45 and told him I was taking the men back to the base, with or without him. I made no overt actions, nor did I threaten him in any way, but he may have gotten that impression. And considering our lack of combat readiness, he may actually have come to the realization that going after Charlie was not a smart move, although I doubt that was the case. Why he didn't push it further didn't matter, the important thing was that we got back to our base without additional casualties

The captain's helicopter got in first, but because he didn't hang around after it landed, I didn't know what he had planned for me, not that I cared. I knew I made the right decision. As it turned out, I not only didn't hear another word about the incident, I never saw him again. But about two weeks later, in mid-December, the company First Sergeant handed me orders transferring me out of Echo Company. I was to report immediately to the Second Brigade Civil Affairs Unit based in An Loc, about 75 miles northeast of Tay Ninh. It was apparent that the captain had no choice but to get rid of me, which was fine with me, even though I felt bad about leaving my squad. My men and I had become as close, or closer, than family, and I never would have been the one to request a transfer. But I knew there was no way the captain and I could remain in the same unit, and since he wasn't going away any time soon, it had to be me. I had no idea what the Civil Affairs Unit was or did, or what my duties would be, but I was optimistic that it would be less stressful and safer than being in the boonies day after day. Yet something kept gnawing away at me about leaving my squad and the rest of Echo Recon. Even though I had no control over my transfer, I felt as though I was abandoning them.

Chapter 13 – Civil Affairs and Psyops

I gathered what little belongings I had and caught a hop on a supply chopper to An Loc. I found the Civil Affairs building, reported in, and was directed to Lieutenant Mellitin, head of the unit. My initial impression of him was not a very positive one, but I was relieved to be out of the field, so I wasn't going to say anything to get me off on the wrong foot with him. Unfortunately, as I got to know him better I realized my first impression was pretty accurate; his leadership style wasn't right for Vietnam. He never asked, he always commanded, and in a very rigid and cocky manner. And no matter what the job, detail, or mission, everything had to be 100% by the book—his book. There could not be the slightest variation even though his book was written for stateside duty, not a war zone. He was totally inflexible, regardless of the circumstances. He had no concept of reality, only what his manuals said. And like too many other career officers in Vietnam, he didn't give a damn about his men, only how their actions and accomplishments could serve as stepping stones to a promotion for him. He was the type of officer who would have gotten people killed if he was in actual combat, unless he got himself killed first. But I still had five months to go, so I did my best to keep a low profile, follow orders, and not make waves. As much as I often wanted to tell him to stick his orders up his ass, I forced myself to stay cool and keep my mouth shut.

The lieutenant gave me a quick rundown of what the Civil Affairs unit was all about and showed me around the area. He introduced me to the four men I would be working closest with—McGaha, Sammy, Scotty, and Chad. All four held the rank of Spec-4 (Specialist 4th Class), so that made me the highest ranking enlisted man in the unit. *Enlisted man* in this context is anyone below officer grade, regardless of whether he enlisted, is a draftee, or a reservist. There were other men in the Civil Affairs unit, but they all worked in various support capacities, supporting our field activities. McGaha and Sammy were actually mechanics and drivers from the brigade motor pool, but they were on permanent loan to the Civil Affairs unit. Scotty was the only one of the four who was officially assigned to Civil Affairs. While Chad did work with us, he was part of the 6th Psyops (Psychological Operations) Battalion. It wasn't until a few days after I arrived that I found out my duties were to include Psyops air missions as well. And working closely with Chad on those missions was what created a strong bond between us. There was even a two-page article about us and our Psyops missions in one of the First Cav's in-country newspapers.

The goal of the army's Civil Affairs effort was *To Seal the Victory* in the so-called secure areas of Vietnam by *Winning the Hearts and Minds of the Vietnamese People.* This was to be accomplished by helping the civilian population in the nearby friendly villages improve the quality of their lives, mainly through Medcaps (Medical Civil Action Programs), humanitarian efforts, and recreational activities, such as movies. While the basic mission of the Psyops effort was similar, it also included leaflet production and distribution, along with live audio broadcasts from the air.

Those propaganda techniques were used in an attempt to persuade the local population to support their nationally elected government, the Government of South Vietnam in Saigon, and to convince the Viet Cong they should surrender and change their loyalties.

I was happy to be out of a combat unit and didn't care that I no longer was a grunt. Actually, from that moment on, the grunts in the field would refer to me as a *REMF* (Rear Echelon Mother Fucker). Even though there were no true safe havens in Vietnam, I initially felt I had a much better chance of survival than I did humping in the boonies. And my living conditions were significantly better than they had been with Echo Recon. I shared a Quonset hut—a lightweight prefabricated structure made of corrugated galvanized steel—with some of the other Civil Affairs guys. My bed was a cot, complete with air mattress and mosquito net, and I ate hot food in the mess tent—no more C-Rats. Three hots and a cot, what more could I ask for? But as I soon realized, feeling safe and actually being safe are often two different things, far removed from one another. Never did I suspect that my life would be more at risk once I was out of the boonies, but that's exactly how I felt every time I left the base on a Civil Affairs or Psyops mission.

When I arrived at Civil Affairs I didn't have a clue as to what my new duties and responsibilities would be, but I never imagined spending my first evening showing an American movie to the local villagers, after dark and in their village, of all places. There were four of us—Scotty, the two guys from the motor pool, and me. A deuce and a half (2-1/2 ton truck) had already been loaded with a movie projector and generator when the lieutenant told me to sign out an M-16 and meet the other guys at the main gate. Scotty and I were to guard the guys, the truck, and the equipment, while Sammy and McGaha set up the screen, projector and audio equipment. Waiting impatiently for us to get the show started were mostly young kids and teenagers, but a lot of adults were just as anxious as the kids for the John Wayne western to start. We were a good distance from the base, in a Vietnamese village at night, with no communications equipment and only two M-16's and a couple of handguns. Yet my three comrades didn't seem at all concerned. If there were any VC around who wanted us dead we would have been, easily. I may have been out of the field, but I certainly wasn't out of danger, not in the least. I felt more vulnerable at that moment than I had at any time in the boonies with Echo Recon. Nothing happened, but that didn't ease my concern or prevent my anxiety level from skyrocketing every time I left the base.

I never ran into problems during any of my trips off the base, but I was much more fearful when we went into one of the villages than I ever had been on a recon mission. With Echo Recon everyone was well armed and prepared for enemy contact. Not so with the Civil Affairs unit. We never had more than two M-16s on any of my off-base missions. The villages we went into were supposed to be friendly, but there was no way to know for sure; even friendly villages had VC among its inhabitants. It's a wonder I was able to keep from firing at anyone I saw dressed in black pajamas and a coolie hat, although I did come close a few times. No matter what I had to do to help with the supplies or equipment, I always had my loaded .45 on my hip. And I hardly ever let go of my M-16, it either was slung over my shoulder or in my hands at all times, with a full magazine and a round in the chamber. And the few times I had to put it down for a moment I made sure it was within easy reach. If we were attacked I wasn't about to go down without a fight.

Out trips to the local villages usually meant traveling through some jungle areas, and even though we went by jeep and truck on roads that were supposed to be safe, I was always nervous. My first Medcap involved taking vaccines and assorted medical supplies to a village about ten klicks from the base. The mission personnel were a doctor, a nurse, one driver, and me. The driver and I each had an M-16 and a .45, and that was it. The doctor and nurse were both unarmed. If we ran into NVA or VC we would have been in deep shit. It was fairly common for the VC to retaliate against villages that showed support for the South Vietnam regime and U.S. forces. And when they did, it wasn't pretty—they usually tortured and then executed the village elder and his family in front of the rest of the villagers. I'm sure if a Medcap, or any other Civil Affairs activity, was in progress when they targeted a village it would have been the end of the line for everyone involved.

I will say that talking to the local villagers gave me a completely different picture of our role in Vietnam, and how we were perceived by the average Vietnamese civilians. Our government told us repeatedly that our presence in Vietnam was to keep the South Vietnamese people free from communist domination, and to prevent the spread of communism to neighboring countries. Stopping the *domino effect* was in our best interest. Yes, we were there to prevent a communist takeover of the government, but not for the sake of the general population. The majority of South Vietnamese people were farmers of one sort or another. They had little formal education, were predominately non-political, and mainly wanted to be left alone. As long as they could put food on their tables and keep roofs over their heads they were satisfied. They knew their lives were not going to change no matter what political group controlled the country, whether it was based on capitalism or communism. All they wanted was for the killing and pillaging to stop so they could live their lives peacefully, yet, as long as we were there that wasn't possible.

The second concern for my safety hit me when the lieutenant called me into his office one morning to explain my additional duties and responsibilities. He told me I would be alternating between the standard Civil Affairs work and *Chiou Hoi* (Chew Hoy), or *Open Arms,* missions that were part of the brigade's Psyops program. That was the program to distribute propaganda to the VC in an attempt to get them to surrender and support the South Vietnamese government. I would be going up in a Huey helicopter equipped with a 1000-watt speaker system hanging from one of the chopper's open doors, and an ARVN (Army of the Republic of Viet Nam) translator who would broadcast the Chiou Hoi messages in Vietnamese. My job was to dump thousands of the surrender leaflets out of the other open door from an altitude of between 500 and 1000 feet. Also on board were the pilot and co-pilot, of course, and two door gunners, one on each side of the chopper. It was obvious from my first Psyops mission that the VC were not very happy to hear our broadcasts and have the county-side littered with propaganda leaflets, as they tried to shoot us down almost every time we went up.

At times we were asked to fly food and supplies from our base to one of the nearby villages, and occasionally from one village to another. Fortunately all of those trips were also uneventful from a safety standpoint, but some had very unexpected results. On one such occasion we had to pick up a shipment of *Nuoc Mam* (Nook Mom) from a nearby village and transport it by chopper to a village some distance away. Nuoc Mam is a Southeastern Asia fish sauce used primarily as an all purpose condiment. The Vietnamese version is prepared by filling large barrels with raw fish, water, sea salt, and a variety of herbs and spices. Today, the raw fish comes mostly from single species, but back then it was whatever the nets of the local fishermen happened to catch. The barrels were then left sitting in the sun for anywhere from one to six months. The resulting liquid from the fermentation process is the fish sauce. Nuoc Mam that has been only briefly fermented has a very pronounced fishy taste and extremely strong odor, while extended fermentation reduces the fishy characteristics and gives the sauce a nuttier flavor. The sauce we transported that day apparently had undergone a very short fermentation because a very small amount spilled onto the floor of the helicopter and no matter how many times or how hard we scrubbed the area, we were never able to get rid of the horrible fish odor. It was so bad that none of the flight crews wanted to go anywhere near that chopper, let alone fly in it.

And then there was the time I went into a village very close to the base for something other than a Civil Affairs mission—lunch. My ARVN interpreter came from that village and on one of the few days that we had no missions scheduled, he invited me to go to the village with him for lunch. He assured me it was perfectly safe, we would both be armed, and the village had no VC living there, so I nervously agreed. After introducing me to his father, mother, two young sisters, and a few villagers, we all sat in a circle on the ground and ate stew his mother served from a large pot sitting on an open fire. I recognized shrimp and a few vegetables, but I couldn't tell what the meat was that was in my bowl. Even though it was quite tasty, I couldn't help wondering if I was eating someone's former house pet, so I didn't dare ask what it was.

My last Psyops mission was the day my chopper got shot down, less than a month before I was scheduled to DEROS. Most of the army chopper pilots in Vietnam were Warrant Officers and as such were addressed as Mister. Mister Planck was one the pilots that flew many of our Psyops missions. I always thought he was very good at his job but never fully realized just how absolutely outstanding a pilot he was until one very frightening day in late April. Occasionally we would find small holes in the choppers as a result of enemy ground fire but up until then I was never in a chopper that had any major damages or suffered casualties. We loaded up the leaflets, tested the speaker system, and took off around mid-morning from one end of the long base runway. There were the usual six of us on board.

The Psyops missions were plotted based on where intelligence reports indicated suspected VC-controlled areas were located, and they were almost always heavily wooded. On that day Mr. Planck did a wide 180-degree turn and climbed to about 500-600 feet as soon as we cleared the base. As the chopper flew parallel to the runway we had taken off from, but in the opposite direction, we started receiving very heavy 50-caliber machine gun fire from the woods below. The loud noise from the engines and rotors normally muffled the sound of ground fire, but anytime our door gunners began firing their machine guns, I knew the enemy was trying to shoot us down. Within seconds after our door gunners started firing on that day, red lights flashed on the cockpit instrument panel, loud beeping noises, like the piercing sound of a smoke alarm, filled the air, and the sound of the engine changed. At least one of those 50-caliber rounds had knocked out our engine. The Huey was designed so the rotor blades could auto-gyrate if the engine loses power, but normally the helicopter has to be at a much higher altitude than we were at for the auto-gyrate to work. We should have fallen out of the sky straight down like a giant rock, but thanks to Mr. Planck's exceptional piloting skills, we didn't. He was pulling up on the control stick that was between his knees while the co-pilot flipped switches on front panel. We were going down pretty fast, but as we were Mr. Planck somehow managed to execute another 180-degree turn and maneuver the chopper around to the opposite end of the runway from which we had taken off. The chopper's skids did hit the ground very hard just as we got to the edge of the runway, and then we bounced a couple of hundred of feet back into the air. This hitting hard and bouncing up continued down the entire length of the runway, with each bounce not as quite as high as the previous one. Mr. Planck brought the chopper to a stop at almost the exact spot we took off from just a few chilling minutes before.

We scrambled off as fast as we could get ourselves moving, wondering if the helicopter might explode any second from the impacts and leaking fuel. The crash crew arrived and immediately hosed down the chopper just in case. As we looked at some pretty big holes in the side of the helicopter we thought it was miraculous it hadn't crashed and burned. Many helicopters did get shot down in Vietnam, and often from much less damage than ours sustained. It was a scary experience and it took quite a while before I calmed down. My mind was filled with my usual questions; was it luck or coincidence, or was someone or something watching over me again? Do we have guardian angels? Are our lives predestined, predetermined? More unanswered questions and more sleepless nights.

The next morning, still shaky from the helicopter incident, I was called in to Lieutenant Mellitin's office. I expected some comment about the chopper incident, but his only remark was that it was a shame we lost a helicopter. He then told me I was scheduled for another Psyops mission later that day. Still reeling from the previous day, I couldn't believe what I was hearing. I told him in no uncertain terms that I not only would not be going on a mission that day, I wasn't going on any Psyops missions during my final three weeks. He promptly went on a long tirade about disobeying orders and threatened me with a court-martial, which got me even angrier. I informed him I also had no intention of doing any Civil Affairs work that required me to leave the base. In fact, the only time I planned on leaving the base was the day I was scheduled to leave Vietnam, period. That brought on a slew of additional threats, none of which I wanted to listen to, so I simply walked out of his office. As I expected, he never followed through with any of his threats and I did my best to stay away from him for the remainder of my time there. I think he also went out of his way to keep a safe distance from me.

The day before my departure I said goodbye to the guys I had worked closely with the previous five months. This left me with very different feelings than I had when I departed Echo Company. I didn't feel I was abandoning them, yet I knew they were still a part of me and I would miss them. I felt very close to them, but it wasn't quite the same as the bond that developed with my combat brothers. Those were truly my brothers, and my comrades from Civil Affairs were more like cousins.

On May 12th, my last day in An Loc, Mr. Planck offered to fly me to Bien Hoa Air Base, where I was to report for out-processing. I said I didn't ever want to get into another helicopter so

I would wait for a seat on one of the transport planes. He was very persistent, saying he had already commandeered a Loach for just that purpose. Loach is the slang name for LOH, a small, two-seat Light Observation Helicopter. Considering he went to such lengths for me, I couldn't say no, but it was the last helicopter ride I ever took.

After checking in at the processing center later that afternoon I was shown where the mess hall was and where I was to spend the night. I had to be back at the center at 0800 hours the next morning for processing. After a fairly decent meal, I spent the night in a bunk with a real mattress, but in spite of the amenities I got very little sleep. It was happiness and nervousness all mixed together. I could not have been more eager to finally be leaving the war behind, but I was worried because even Bien Hoa experienced rocket attacks from time to time, and I knew guys got killed on their last day in country. As close as I was to getting out of there, I wasn't able to relax, not even a little.

The following morning, after an early breakfast of real scrambled eggs, not powdered, I was back at the processing center, impatiently waiting for my turn to get started and finally get the hell out of there. It took the better part of the morning to finish, including exchanging my few MPCs back into greenbacks, and then there was nothing to do but wait. There I was, ten months, three weeks, and two days after arriving in Viet Nam, alive and well, sitting on the ground, waiting for the *Freedom Bird* that was going to fly me and a couple of hundred other guys back to T*he World*. But was I truly well? On the outside I may have been the same Howard Patrick, but I knew on the inside I was a very different person from the green FNG who arrived almost a year earlier. I sat there thinking back to the day I arrived in Vietnam and the men I saw sitting around just staring into space. I was now one of them, a battle-weary warrior with the *thousand yard stare* I had seen on so many faces that first day.

A Continental Airlines plane finally landed and taxied to the same spot as the one I arrived on. Cheers went up from many of those waiting to leave, but not from me. And not from quite a few others who were sitting with blank expressions on their faces. When we finally boarded the plane I was still tense and jittery, but once we were in the air and the cheering died down the anxiety slowly began to ease up. It was replaced with feelings of an entirely different nature that are hard to express.

Chapter 14 – Back to The World

As the plane lifted off the ground, the cabin filled with an eruption of cheers, hollers, shouts, and whistles that seemed to pump life back into my weary body and mind. I had literally gone through hell and survived, bringing on emotions that were unlike any I had experienced before, or since. Certainly I was happy beyond belief that I had made it out alive, but at the same time I couldn't stop wondering about the comrades I left behind. My squad from Echo Recon—did they get out unscathed? Are the guys okay? What about the rest of Echo Recon—any casualties since I left them? Any I knew? How about the men I worked with in Civil Affairs? How's my buddy Chad from Psyops? In a strange way a part of me was not happy that I left. It's hard to explain the bond that develops between men in war to anyone whose closest contact with real war is books and movies. I felt closer to some of those men than I did to my closest friends, even to family members, and a part of me felt that I still should be there with them. If I was, maybe my presence would help them make it home and possibly prevent some of them from becoming casualties. Then again, if I were still there maybe I would be the one to become a casualty. I finally forced myself to put all thoughts aside as I shut my eyes and drifted off into the closest thing to a restful sleep that I had experienced in a very long time.

Just like my flight to Vietnam, the plane made a refueling stop in Hawaii, but this time when we disembarked we had access to a section of the terminal. During the flight we had been served typical airline food but no alcoholic drinks, so it wasn't surprising that many of the guys came back from the terminal a little tipsy—a few more than a little. When we finally landed in Oakland we had to go through customs before getting bused to the processing center. We had been told during out-processing that almost any type of military weapons we tried to bring home as souvenirs—guns, rifles, knives, bayonets—would be confiscated during the customs check, so I didn't even try to bring anything like that back. All I had were my boonie hat, a cold-weather cap, a Zippo lighter engraved with a First Cav insignia, and a First Cav commemorative coin.

Once at the center we were separated into two groups, those being reassigned to new duty stations and my group, those getting discharged from active duty. My group was taken into a very large room with floor-to-ceiling bleacher-type seats along one wall, numbered desks in the center, and floor markers to direct us from one station to the next. The room was at least double the size of a basketball stadium. We were called down from the bleachers one at a time, by name, and directed to desk number one, the first of the many stations we had to process through. They included one where I was measured for a new dress-green uniform and one where I met with a re-enlistment officer who tried to convince me to stay in the army. Once again, OCS was the main carrot he used to entice me, but he couldn't offer me enough to re-up. I survived Vietnam once and there was no way I would intentionally put myself in a position that might put me right back there. The normal amount of time in service for a draftee was a total of six years—two years active duty, followed by four years in the active reserves, but those of us who were in combat could choose being in the inactive reserves for those remaining four years. While there was still the possibility of being recalled to active duty, there were no monthly meetings and no two-week summer camps to attend. It took me all of two seconds to decide on inactive reserves, and I received my Honorable Discharge exactly four years later.

At another station I was given a medical exam to make sure I had no health issues and was well enough to be discharged. The exam consisted of height, weight, temperature, and blood pressure measurements; about a page worth of questions to answer; and a so-called mental evaluation. I mentioned my ankle injury and the fact that it would always be weak. Much to my surprise the doctor went ahead and put me in for a ten-percent disability rating. Although it didn't amount to much money, I was not about to turn it down. The monthly checks began a few months after my discharge and continued for two years, until I was called in to the VA hospital for a re-evaluation. That examination, if it can even be called that, was a real joke. The doctor had me take off both shoes and socks, wiggle both ankles, and then put my socks and shoes back on. That was it. About a month later I received a letter from the VA informing me that the doctor's report indicated my ankle was fine. My disability rating was being removed effective immediately and I would no longer receive the monthly checks. I was pretty pissed off about it, but I never thought to dispute it and request a review. I was actually happy to be done with any part of the military, hopefully forever.

Another station was finance, where I was told I had to reimburse Uncle Sam for being paid during my 30-day emergency leave. The fact that I had told them not to pay me for that leave was irrelevant. Things like that were all too common in the military. I could have sent them a check from the money Judy saved, but I was so annoyed at the way the situation was mishandled I decided to drag out the repayment as long as I could. The smallest monthly amount they would accept was $10 so that's what they got, starting three months later. As it turned out the monthly disability payments I received more than covered the payback amount, somewhat easing my annoyance over the whole situation.

Because Judy was living with her parents, she was able to save a good portion of my salary every month. Our hope was to accumulate enough for a down payment on a house. We wanted to be out of her parent's house and on our own again as soon as possible, but we didn't want to go back to an apartment first and move again later. In fact, I purposely didn't take the one-week R & R (Rest and Recuperation) I was entitled to while in 'Nam. We had decided it would be better for us in the long run to put the money toward a house instead of airfare and a hotel in Hawaii. As it was the most popular R & R destination for married couples, I'm sure that's where we would have gone.

As soon as I finished the processing, I boarded a military shuttle bus to Oakland International Airport. I had $25 in my pocket and a travel voucher for a flight to Philadelphia. It had to be obvious to almost everyone in the terminal that I had just returned from

'Nam. I was wearing my new dress green uniform, with a First Cav patch on one shoulder, a blue infantry braid over the other shoulder, and ribbons on my chest—Vietnam Service Medal, Air Medal, CIB (Combat Infantry Badge), and Bronze Star. I wasn't expecting a band or a parade, but I also wasn't expecting to be avoided like I had the plague. Yet that was my experience. Almost everyone near me stared constantly as though I carried a sign saying *Dangerous – Keep Away!* I knew the war had become increasingly unpopular with the public, but I didn't expect everyone to take it out on us — the soldiers. During my time in 'Nam I was aware of the protest demonstrations throughout the country. What I wasn't aware of was that the majority of those opposed to the war didn't just blame the government for getting our country involved; they blamed us, the soldiers, for our participation in it. They acted as though we were responsible for starting the war and keeping it going. It didn't matter that hundreds and thousands of soldiers who responded to the government's call to duty were dying at an alarming rate. In the eyes of the public it was as though we were the enemy and the draft dodgers were the heroes. We got shit on and the guys who burned their draft cards and fled the country were treated like celebrities.

Fellow returning veterans related some of their experiences to me, and most were not very pretty. Just going from their processing centers to the local airports, many had eggs thrown at them, were spit on, and were called every derogatory name you could think of. The worst, yet most common, was being called *baby killer*. Fortunately, my treatment at the airport was limited to avoidance, stares, whispers, and people getting up and leaving their seats when I sat close to them. I know if I had been spit on or had eggs thrown at me I would not have let it go peacefully. Even though I was a draftee and certainly didn't want to go to Vietnam, I was proud of having served my country, and anyone disrespecting me, my uniform, or my country would have been in for an unpleasant surprise. Years later I saw a PBS documentary about Medal of Honor recipients. A former Army Captain was asked what his life was like after returning home from Vietnam. With a very soft, cracking voice, and tears trickling down his cheeks, he said, *"The military turned us into loaded weapons, and then sent us home without ever unloading us."* Tens of thousands of ordinary, decent, civilized young men were molded into hardened, unemotional, cold-blooded killers. And when our jobs were done, we were simply abandoned, left to deal with the lasting effects of our war-time exposure totally on our own. That was me, a loaded weapon, cocked and ready to fire. Luckily, there were no incidents on the plane ride to Philadelphia that might have caused me to explode.

For almost the entire previous year all I thought about was getting out of Vietnam alive, and there I was, finally home. I was among the fortunate ones. I had made it home in one piece. A few scrapes, scratches, bruises, and the weak ankle, but, all in all, I was in pretty good shape. At least that's what I thought at the time. World War I had its *shell-shock* casualties, World War II and Korea their *battle fatigue*, but those disorders weren't supposed to happen to soldiers in Vietnam. Our military and mental health experts had theorized that those psychological wounds developed because of prolonged time spent in a war zone. They were confident that limiting the Vietnam tour of duty to a year would dramatically reduce the probability of soldiers developing what is now referred to as post traumatic stress disorder (PTSD). And that's how the one-year Vietnam tour of duty was established.

It was not until the late 1970s, well after we were out of Vietnam, that the VA (Department of Veterans Affairs) finally accepted PTSD as a medical reality. In fact, that was when the term PTSD was first coined. We now know that even a single exposure to a traumatic event can be enough to cause some individuals to develop post-traumatic stress. And studies have shown that the brain actually undergoes permanent chemical changes as a result of repeated exposure to the same type of traumatic events, with no known means of reversal. It was that constant day-after-day exposure to the trauma of combat that resulted in such large numbers of combat veterans developing some degree of post-traumatic stress.

Some combat vets undergo major transformations, others experience only minor changes, but all have been altered in some way, even though many of us were not aware it was happening. We didn't realize we were subconsciously doing things that enabled us to get through each day without reliving the painful memories of war. We were instinctively avoiding the things that might trigger those memories, and if that didn't work, we often self-medicated ourselves with drugs and alcohol. We often isolated ourselves, even from the people we had been very close to before the war. And even then, we thought our actions were perfectly normal—it was everyone else who were fucked up.

On the outside I may have appeared to be just fine, but inside I had become an emotionally numb, combat-hardened warrior with anxiety, anger, and survivor guilt issues. And like many physical wounds, the psychological scars of war never fully disappear. They may improve, as was the case with me, but they never go away entirely. As one Vietnam vet said to his mother when she told him he wasn't acting like the son she knew, *"mom, the son you knew died in Vietnam, someone else returned in his place."*

I knew the war had changed me, but didn't realize the extent of those changes. I came back in better physical shape than I was in before Vietnam, so I was sure I would be my old self in no time. Looking back, and knowing what I know now about PTSD, I certainly had many of the classic combat-induced symptoms of the disorder. But the mind is an amazing thing. It not only controls our bodies, it often finds ways to protect us from ourselves. It can help us deal with tragedies and traumatic events by blocking out memories that might otherwise be much too painful to deal with, or even live with. And that's often the case with many combat vets. If the memories that cause us pain are buried so deep in our subconscious that it's as though they never existed, then the pain would not exist either. That was me. As my Vietnam memories got buried deeper and deeper, my pain and torment subsided.

Chapter 15 – Home At Last

On the afternoon of May 14th I landed at Philadelphia International Airport and was greeted by my wife, daughter, parents, and sister. We all hugged and kissed and shed tears of happiness, except for Ellen. She had been fine until I held out my arms for her to come to me. She turned away and began crying, loud and hard. I'm sure she was wondering who this stranger is and why is he trying to grab me. The crying didn't last, fortunately, and it wasn't long before she warmed up to me. Then it was as if we had never been separated. In fact, she seemed to have waited for my return before taking her first steps on her own. She must have known how happy that would make me, and it certainly did.

My parents had flags and welcome-home signs hanging in front of their house when I got back, and a few days after my return they threw a homecoming party for me. Some of my close relatives and old friends were there, but I kept thinking that I no longer had anything in common with any of them. I even wondered what I was doing there. Everyone was eating, drinking, laughing, and having a wonderful time, except me. They talked non-stop about their petty little problems and material possessions, and I wondered how they could possibly think such trivial things were important. Hardly anyone talked to me and I don't think I said more than a few words to any of them. The whole party was ridiculously stupid and I felt a need to be away from it all, so I went to my old bedroom until everyone left. I doubt that I was even missed. Sitting there in the dark all I could think about was how much so many Americans take for granted—everyday things like running water, hot showers, indoor toilets, clean clothes to wear, even having enough food to eat. I promised myself that I would never get caught up in all the materialistic bullshit that seemed to consume everyone at the party.

I wasn't ready to go back to IBM yet, so I spent the summer trying to readjust to life with my family, friends, and the changes in my living conditions. I thought it would be a relatively easy transition, but it was harder than I expected. I was in a constant state of vigilance, and my anxiety level was almost as high as it had been in Vietnam. I didn't want to give Judy cause for concern, so I worked hard to hide my uneasiness. In many ways I felt like I was back in 'Nam, always cautious, always on guard, and ready to act in the event of trouble. I silently evaluated the likely threat potential of almost everyone I came in contact with, and always had an escape plan in the event I had to make a hasty exit from wherever I was. So maybe my uncharacteristic behavior toward other people played a role in their feelings towards me, although at the time such a possibility wouldn't have entered my mind. After all, I didn't have any real problems or issues; I was just a bit cautious about the potential danger from any and all sources, as my training and combat experience had taught me to be. That didn't mean there was anything wrong with me, did it?

From the day I returned home, I had one negative experience after another, constantly reinforcing my belief that the majority of my countrymen despised Vietnam veterans. Almost 60,000 soldiers lost their lives in Vietnam, and thousands more came home with serious physical and mental disabilities. Instead of showing respect for them and the sacrifices they made, the general public's attitude was that they got everything they deserved. To this day, many still believe that in spite of their enjoyment of freedoms made possible by our soldiers' sacrifices. Shortly after returning to work at IBM I ran into one of the guys I had worked with before Vietnam. He gave me a friendly greeting, shook my hand, and asked where I had been hiding, as he hadn't seen me in a very long time. When I mentioned Vietnam he reacted as though I had a contagious disease. He immediately dropped my hand, backed up a few steps, and made a lame excuse about being late for a meeting. As he turned away he muttered something like "it was good seeing you again Howard." Sure, I said to myself, I'll probably never see him again, and I never did. Once other co-workers heard I had been in Vietnam, their attitudes changed as well; they went from friendly and talkative to quiet and reserved. Many of the people I met socially did the same thing, friendly and talkative until Vietnam was mentioned, followed by an awkward silence and an excuse to get away from me. A few people asked a question or two, but the only one that sticks in my mind was from a friend of a relative who wanted to know how many people I had killed. That was the day I not only stopped telling people I was a Vietnam veteran, I even stopped mentioning I had ever been in the army.

But not talking about being in the service didn't prevent me from overhearing people speaking of Vietnam veterans as crazed baby-killers. Of course the public's anti-military attitude was fueled in part by the media's continuous supply of misleading stories about atrocities by our soldiers. It was not easy to keep my cool when I heard those comments, but even more infuriating was hearing guys talk about how they had dodged the draft. I don't mean the ones who were lucky enough not to get called up or those who had legitimate medical reasons for being ineligible. I'm talking about the guys who used dishonest means to get disqualified; like faking homosexuality or using trumped-up health issues to get deferments.

A few years after I returned to civilian life a neighbor invited me to a weekly poker game, and I became a regular. The neighbor and three of the other players were Philadelphia school teachers and had been friends since college. On this particular occasion, the four of them complained all night about how much they hated their jobs. Not their salaries, not the hours or travel time, not the schools they taught in, not their principals—they simply hated teaching. It came out that they had become teachers for one reason and one reason only—to avoid the draft. They knew Vietnam would be a real possibility for them once they graduated from college and lost their school exemptions, but because teachers were exempt from the draft they decided that was their ticket out of military service. If they had a real passion to become teachers it certainly would have been okay in my book. I believe the more truly dedicated teachers we have, the better, but that wasn't the case with those guys, just the opposite. They had no more interest in teaching than I had in re-enlisting in the army—probably a lot less. All they cared about was staying out of Vietnam, regardless of the means used and the negative effects their attitudes might have on their students. It didn't matter to them that they didn't give a damn about the kids they taught. It didn't matter that they were not motivated to help prepare their students for life's challenges. They had no business ever becoming teachers. I was fuming inside, but I forced myself to stay quiet. I was fearful that I might say something that could lead to a physical fight, and I knew if that happened I wouldn't be satisfied until someone was hurt, and it would not have been me. That was the last time I was able to play cards with them.

In September I returned to IBM, expecting to stay with the company until I retired. That was my feeling when I originally accepted the job, and I didn't think my two-year absence would change that. The government had required medium to large corporations to take back employees that had been drafted, put them in the same or similar positions they held before going into the service, and increase their salaries to the same levels they would have been making had they not been drafted. When I returned to IBM, I did go back to my old job and I did get a raise, but it was much smaller than I felt it should have been. Of course my manager disagreed with me, but I didn't put up too much of an argument for fear I would lose the job. I was pissed, but I wanted to stay with IBM.

I was apprehensive as to how the absence would affect my performance, but it didn't take me long to get back into the swing of things. I was surprised at how quickly I readjusted to fixing computers. Maybe it was because computers are not people, and I didn't have to engage in conversations with them and listen to their petty complaints. It took a while, but eventually I reached a point where I felt my life had returned to a reasonable level of normalcy, although my actions and behavior said otherwise. The signs that I was dramatically different from the person I had been before Vietnam were there all along, but unrecognized by me. Anger and isolation were the most prominent indicators. I would get pissed off over stupid little things that never upset me before. And I was isolating myself more and more by burying myself in work. In the same way other people put up invisible barriers between themselves and me, I did much the same thing in reverse. As much as possible I avoided contact with people in general, which all too often included my family.

A few months after my son Eric was born, the company sent me to Chicago for six weeks of training on a new model computer. They were paying my travel expenses and per diem for food and lodging, so Judy and I decided we should all go so we wouldn't be separated for so long. We packed up the kids, loaded the car, and headed west. IBM provided a list of short-term furnished apartments and we found one a block from an elevated train line like we have in Philadelphia, which I used to go to the training center every day. It wasn't until the course started that I found out I would be changing shifts every two weeks—first was 8 a.m. to 4 p.m.—then 4 p.m. to midnight—and finally midnight to 8 a.m. The first four weeks weren't too bad, but I got almost no sleep at all during the last two weeks. The kids were already up when I got back to the apartment, and it was hard to sleep through their usual noisiness, along with the normal daytime sounds from outside. I was irritable the entire six weeks, but I wrote it off to the shift changes and being in a different living environment. I seemed to be able to come up with acceptable reasons to write off all the Post Traumatic Stress symptoms I was exhibiting, without a single thought to the possibility they could be Vietnam related.

When I got back from Chicago, I received another small salary increase and I did get overtime anytime I worked more than a 7-1/2 hour day. While I was away, the office had set up a rotational on-call schedule for handling second and third shift service calls, which also meant extra pay when I was the on-call tech. While the overtime pay and on-call differential certainly improved my overall compensation, I was still angry over the meager raise when I returned, and that anger continued eating away at me.

Normally I worked on the new system I had just been trained on and it didn't take me long to become very good at troubleshooting and repairing just about any problem I was faced with. But during the weeks I was the on-call CE I was required to be the first responder to any problem that came in; even if it was on equipment I was not trained on. As far as I was concerned a computer was a computer and within the IBM family of computers there were many similarities. I knew I could apply my training to any IBM computer so I was never afraid to tackle a problem on machines I had never seen before. The worst thing that might happen was I wouldn't be able to fix it, but most of the time I did.

The entire next year I literally worked my ass off. If I was asked to stay on a call after my normal quitting time, I did. If I was asked to work on a Saturday or Sunday, I did. And no matter what I was asked to work on, I did it, including equipment I was not trained on. Many of my co-workers refused to work on anything they were unfamiliar with, but not me. I thought it was because of my determination to be the best CE the Philadelphia office ever had. I wanted to do all I could to show my boss I deserved a promotion and the appropriate salary increase that would go along with it. Or, so I thought. Looking back, I'm sure it was another symptom of PTSD. I continued to use work to isolate myself, and it kept getting worse as time went on.

It had been quite some time since I had a performance review, so I requested a meeting with my manager. He listened to my reasons why I should be promoted to Senior Customer Engineer. He ended our meeting by telling me he would look into it and get back to me. About a week later we had the follow-up meeting, but even before it was over I knew my days at IBM were numbered. It also made me realize how volatile I had become. He said I was doing a good job and the company had great long term plans for me, but there was no promotion, not even a small raise, in my immediate future, and he couldn't give me any idea of when I could expect those things to happen. He said I should just hang in there and ultimately I would be very happy with my progress in the company.

Management had great plans for me. When I tried to get some sense of what those plans were, he was evasive. All he said was it would happen and I would be very pleased with it. I wasn't happy with my salary when I returned to the company after the army, and this runaround soured my attitude toward IBM even more. The more he talked, the angrier I became. I actually felt like punching him out, but when those thoughts turned to doing him even more harm, I was afraid of doing something I would really be sorry for. If I didn't get out of there fast I knew I would be in big trouble. Somehow, I forced myself to leave the office without getting physical. After I calmed down I knew I would be parting ways with IBM as soon as I could find a new job. I also realized I was a powder keg, able to explode without warning, and that was a scary feeling. I actually wondered what would have happened if I had been carrying a gun at the time. I wanted to believe I would not have used it, but I wasn't able to convince myself. I knew if I ever pulled a gun on someone that person would die, so I decided right then and there that owning a handgun was out for me. I never again wanted to be in a situation where I might take the life of an innocent civilian.

Chapter 16 – Riding Life's Roller Coaster

I never had to go out and search for a job, so I thought it might take a while to find the right one for me. As it turned out, technicians with IBM training and experience were in more demand than I realized, and it took no time at all to make the change. My first interview was for a Consulting Engineer (another fancy title for a computer technician) with Computer Hardware Consultants and Services (CHCS) in a nearby Philadelphia suburb. I was offered the job on the spot and I accepted on the spot. The company was started a few years earlier by former IBM employees to provide a full range of technical services to owners of IBM equipment, mainly leasing companies that rented out IBM computers at lower rates than IBM charged. Most of the work involved system upgrades and installations, some of which were done at the company's facility. The majority of the work, however, had to be done at the end-user locations, wherever they happened to be. Although I hadn't done very much of that type of work with IBM, it didn't take long for me to become comfortable with my new job.

As my manager became more confident in my technical abilities, I began doing a lot of traveling, some nearby and some nationally. There were even a number of jobs that took me out of the country, including Canada, Europe, Scandinavia, and South America. And the amount of time away from home never seemed to bother me. In fact, I would usually get so wrapped up in the job at hand I would often forget about calling Judy to let her know when I would be coming home. There were even times when a planned one-day job took two or more days to complete, and I never let Judy know I wouldn't be home as scheduled until I was on my way home. Whenever that occurred, she would tell me how much she worried about me and how inconsiderate I was of her, and she was right on both counts. I always apologized and said it wouldn't happen again, but it did—many times. I would just shrug it off, saying I was so focused on getting the job done that I lost track of time. I never realized I was subconsciously isolating myself, unaware that my anxiety level was lowest and I felt most relaxed when I was by myself—away from people.

Four years after I started working for CHCS, Judy and I decided to move to South Florida. After experiencing southern Florida weather in mid-winter, I was hooked. It was about 80 degrees in Florida when we boarded the plane to Philadelphia and in the low twenties when we landed, with heavy winds and snow everywhere. Less than a year later we were living in Sunrise, Florida and I was a Tech Specialist for a Fort Lauderdale computer manufacturer. However, after only eight months, I changed jobs again, this time back to work on IBM computers for Sorbus, another computer service company. I stayed with that company for about two years, leaving to become a technical instructor for a suburban Cleveland company—Total Technical Services. I continued living in Florida, did my prep work at home, and traveled to Ohio about once every two months to teach two or four-week classes. In that job, I taught other technicians how to maintain and repair different models of IBM computer systems. At a time when it was commonplace for employees to stay with the same company for 20 or more years I had already worked for four different companies, without ever once giving a thought as to what really may have been behind so many changes in such a short period of time. Once again, undetected PTSD was a driving force in my life.

About two years later, the company made it known that it wanted to expand into new areas that were compatible with its core business, and would welcome any employee suggestions. My proposal, because of the expanding electronics and computer industry in South Florida, was to open a private technical school to train entry-level technicians in Fort Lauderdale. After submitting documentation to support the viability for such a school, the company not only decided to go ahead with it, they put me in charge of making it happen. Within six months a building was found and renovated, training equipment and office furnishings were in place, instructors and office staff had been hired, and lesson plans had been created. Total Technical Institute (TTI) was fully licensed by the Florida State Department of Education to teach a nine-month course in Computer Technology, and I was made the school's director. By midway through the third year of operation the school had a positive cash flow, and had received approval for national accreditation and all available state and federal financial aid programs. Enrollment was continuously rising, and things were going well.

I was happy with my job and had no thoughts of leaving, but that changed the day my boss flew in from Cleveland with grim news. The school was making a reasonable profit for the company, but because other areas of the company were losing money at an alarming rate major cutbacks were planned, including employee reductions. He decided that one of the employees to go would be me, and he would be moving to Florida to take over my position as school director. I was floored. In spite of my job hopping, I had never been fired. I had always considered my boss a friend, but I think that may have been his plan right from the moment I talked to him about opening a school in Florida—using me to get it started and on a solid financial foundation, then dumping me so he could it take over.

After my anger subsided enough to think rationally, and after much struggling over what to do next, I thought about opening my own tech school and spent almost a year trying to make that happen. I came close but fell short getting enough financial backing to pull it off. From the time I was let go from TTI, a New Jersey computer training company had been trying to hire me and get me to move back up north. I didn't want to move again but all of our savings had been depleted and I had to do something to earn money again. I was able to negotiate an arrangement to work for them as a private contractor, going to New Jersey only when needed to teach a class, and getting paid a flat rate plus expenses for each class I taught. I continued doing that until the fall of 1981, when I received a phone call from CHCS. They were interested in opening a tech school like TTI in the Philadelphia area and wanted to talk about having me open and run it. I met with the company president the next time I went to New Jersey, and we discussed what he was looking for, what I had accomplished at TTI, and what my requirements would be to start a similar school for his company. In addition to a good starting salary and benefits package, I told him I wanted to be given a percentage of ownership, receive quarterly bonuses based on the school's profits, and have my moving expenses paid for. He agreed to it all, and within a month I was back in the Philadelphia suburbs.

My initial task was to find a suitable building to house the new school. I located, and the company purchased, an old elementary school building just outside of Philadelphia. We named it C-H-I Institute. I had the facility remodeled to meet our needs, hired a staff, created lesson plans and operating procedures, purchased training equipment, and had C-H-I licensed by the state Department of Education in April of 1982. We were initially approved to teach a nine-month course in Computer Technology, very similar to the program I established at TTI. By the end of our first year of operation the school was at a financial breakeven point and continuously made a profit from that time on. My boss was so pleased he gave me a significant raise, leased a company car for me, and even gave me an interest-free loan that enabled Judy and I to buy a house not too far from the school. I truly felt I had finally found the career and the company that I would stay with for the duration of my working years. No more job hopping for me.

On the school's two-year anniversary I submitted an application for national accreditation, which was approved in record time, as was approval for government financial aid availability for the students. The following year the school received approval to teach a 24-month Associate Degree program in Computer Engineering Technology, which included a module on robotics technology. C-H-I was the first technical school in Pennsylvania to get an Associate Degree approval the first time around, and the first tech school in the state to teach robotic technology. The school was thriving, had gained a great reputation, and I was getting involved with a number of trade and technical school associations. I was even participating on national accreditation review teams around the country. I once again felt life was good, as I did when I began my new job at IBM almost 20 years prior. And never could I have envisioned that my life was once again about to take a devastating turn for the worse.

Chapter 17 –Emerging Memories

After the disturbing phone call from Chad in the summer of 1985, I spent the subsequent months trying to remember him and my other buried memories, not only at night, but also during most of my waking hours. Although I did remember much of my first year in the army, everything after getting to Echo Company was still a blank. The dreams about the helicopter incident continued on a fairly regular basis, but nothing else came to mind. The harder I tried to remember, the more frustrated I became. It was agonizing. Then one day, while sitting wide awake at my desk, I had what could only be described as a flashback. I was back in Vietnam, in the middle of a firefight, and it was as just real as when it originally happened. It was dusk but the thick jungle canopy blocked much of the remaining light. I was on my stomach, my rifle leaning on a large fallen tree branch that I was using for cover, firing short bursts at the gun flashes up ahead. A number of VC had walked into our ambush and were firing back at us. When one of the guys in my squad fired his grenade launcher at them the enemy fire stopped, but we didn't know if they were wounded, dead, or maybe even escaped the ambush and took off. I didn't know how many were there when it started, and how many might still be there waiting for us to show ourselves. We played a short waiting game and then fired a few rounds into the area they were shooting from, with no further return fire. One of the guys had to check out the area, and was just about to, when I snapped out of my flashback, sweaty and trembling, just like I was when I woke up from the helicopter dreams.

Over the following weeks, a few memories of Chad slowly popped into my head, and I finally remembered a few guys from the Civil Affairs unit and some of the events I experienced with them. During the months that followed there were new dreams, more memories, and random flashbacks, regardless of where I happened to be and with no clue as to what triggered them. I could be walking down the street and all of a sudden I was back in the boonies—on patrol, setting up an ambush, or right in the middle of a firefight. They were as real as when the events actually happened and it always scared the hell out of me. I was lucky in one respect; I never had a flashback while I was driving, at least not that I remember. The door had been unlocked to memories my mind kept buried for many years, and now it was as though that door was being pushed slowly open and those forgotten recollections began to trickle out.

Chad and I had developed a pretty tight bond during the five months we worked together. And while I was nervous as hell during every one of my Psyops missions, I have no recollection of anything other than positive experiences with him. Of course, the time my helicopter got shot down was quite traumatic, but Chad was not a part of that mission, so I don't think he was the actual trigger that unlocked my closed memory door. It was strictly me and my determination to remember him that forced it open. I'm quite sure if I never got Chad's phone call some other event would have had resulted in the same outcome.

And it certainly was not that I suddenly remembered every detail of my Vietnam experiences. It was a slow progression with bits and pieces popping into my consciousness randomly. Sometimes I would be sitting at my desk at work or watching a TV show at home and all of a sudden I would get a glimpse of something from Vietnam. A few of the things I remembered or dreamt about were not unpleasant memories, but most were a reliving of traumatic events all over again. I was having nightmares and flashbacks, with no way to know when they would turn on and no ability to prevent them from happening. Most times they were repeats of previous dreams and flashbacks, but every so often something new would emerge, and a new series of nightmares would begin. Even now, in spite of how much I do remember, a lot remains jumbled, and there's more that still remain buried somewhere deep down in my subconscious.

As the dreams, nightmares and flashbacks became more frequent, my ability to concentrate and stay focused kept diminishing. I was losing interest in many of the things that had been important to me, and I found myself getting much more easily annoyed over little things for no apparent reason. I got angry with people for simply glancing in my direction or accidentally bumping into me in a crowded store. I was doing the same things I had done in those early days after Vietnam. I was constantly thinking about ways to defend myself in the event I was provoked or attacked. And the first thing I did when entering a store or restaurant was to plan an escape route in case I needed to get out fast. My level of anxiety was higher than ever and I began having frequent panic attacks. I was losing control. I felt like there was a bomb inside of me just waiting to be detonated.

On one occasion I was driving south on I-95 toward downtown Philadelphia. I was in the left lane when a car next to me sped up a little and then moved in front of me without signaling that he was about to change lanes. He really wasn't very close and there was no reason for me to be annoyed, but I was. And not just a little bit, I was raging mad. It was road rage to the extreme. I was only a few miles from my exit, but instead of getting off I stayed dangerously close behind the other driver. When he changed lanes I did also, with one thought in my mind: running him off the road. I think it was seeing the *Welcome to Delaware* sign as I crossed the state line that finally snapped me out of my frenzy. I pulled over to the shoulder of the road and stopped. My heart was racing wildly, and even though it was winter I was sweating profusely. I sat there for over an hour until I calmed down enough to safely drive again. I had totally lost control and didn't know what to do about it, so I did nothing—except to hope it wouldn't happen again. Unfortunately, that wasn't to be, but at least those episodes were much less intense and luckily did not lead to anything harmful happening to anyone.

Before my Vietnam memories surfaced I was happy with my job, my position with the company, and my relationship with my boss. I had job security, financial stability, and was well respected within the proprietary school industry. However, as my anxiety increased my productivity at work steadily decreased. My ability to concentrate and stay focused on the requirements of running the school nosedived. I had always worked on things as soon as they crossed my desk and handled problems as soon as I became aware of them. But I found myself either starting things and never finishing them, or never even starting them in the first place. My desk, which I had always kept neat and orderly, became a mountainous mess. I tried to keep it all together, but I wasn't coming close. Nothing I did to get myself back on track worked. In fact, the harder I tried the worse things became. I no longer seemed to care about work or anything else that had been important to me.

I had always prided myself on my ability to maintain good working relationships with all the people I worked with—whether they were bosses, peers, or subordinates. At C-H-I, my door was always open to both staff and students, for whatever issues they felt a need to discuss. But as time went on I found myself paying much less attention to them. I no longer cared about anyone else's problems. An example was when I fired someone who had become a close friend. He was originally hired as a night school electronics instructor, and I eventually added evening school coordinator to his responsibilities. As we got to know each other better we became good friends, as did our wives and sons. Our common connection was the military—he had been in the Marine Corps for eight years before he went out on a medical discharge. He was a good instructor, and he did a very good job of running the evening school, but there had been a few complaints about his strong managerial style. That was probably a result of being in the marines. Instead of discussing those complaints with him, or even looking closer into them, I removed him from the coordinator position. And when he complained, saying there was nothing to support my action, I fired him. Just like that, and it didn't bother me in the least. I gave no thought whatsoever to how my actions could be harming people—I didn't care. It was like Vietnam: I was emotionally numb. I'll never know how many other lives I messed up, and it bothers the hell out of me. Even though I know my actions were influenced by PTSD, I feel guilty and embarrassed. I can only hope that those I've hurt get to read my story and find it in their hearts to forgive me.

One day I was contacted by a local head hunter who told me that a New York business school owner wanted to open a Philadelphia branch and was interested in talking to me about heading it up. I had been previously contacted by others regarding similar situations, but since I had absolutely no desire to make any kind of employment change, it never progressed past the inquiring phone call. This time, however, I did meet with the school owner, he did offer me the job of opening his new branch and be its director, and I said I would think it over. I normally took time to analyze all the pros and cons before making important decisions, but in this case I accepted without giving it very much thought. I didn't think about what I would be giving up, I only hoped a new challenge might invigorate me and get me refocused and enthused about work again.

When I turned in my resignation my boss was taken completely by surprise. He knew, of course, that my work performance had not been up to par lately, but based on how well a job I had done overall, he thought if I was having a real problem I would have come to him with it. And because of that I couldn't bring myself to tell him the real reason for leaving. Even though I knew he would ask why I was quitting, I didn't have a planned response, so I just said it was a better opportunity, and left it at that. I knew he didn't believe me, but he didn't try to talk me out of it. We made all the necessary arrangements and I was gone before the week was over.

I stayed with the business school for only a year. I was enthused at first, but once I got the school up and running I again began losing interest in what I was doing. So I quit that job and went to work as director of another business school in Philadelphia. That one also lasted only a short time, followed by school director jobs with an electronics school in Northern New Jersey that I commuted to daily, and a truck-driving school in Philadelphia. By that time I was totally confused and frustrated. I had completely lost any desire to stay in the school business or even go back to a teaching position. I didn't want to do anything involving electronics in any capacity, but I didn't have a clue as to what exactly I should do. I really wanted to do nothing at all, but I forced myself to keep looking for something—anything that might get me stimulated again. And through it all the nightmares and flashbacks continued their never-ending attack.

In the hopes that a totally new challenge might help me get me back on track, I decided to give sales management a try. As a school director, a big part of my responsibilities was student enrollment, which was overseeing the admissions department—basically a sales department. Even though it was not direct product sales, I felt it had given me sufficient knowledge and experience to be a sales manager. I took a job with a local start-up prepaid legal service company, set up most of the operational and sales procedures, but insufficient financial reserves led to the company folding before reaching a positive cash flow. That was followed by an inside sales position for a New York City collection company, selling cemetery plots in Philadelphia, mausoleum crypts in a St. Louis suburb, cemetery plots again, that time in Lancaster, Pennsylvania, and finally collection services again for a New Jersey start-up company. None of them lasted a full year. With each job change my income decreased, and as it did our credit card debt climbed. I had finally reached bottom. The credit cards were maxed out and we had almost no money coming in. No other options were available, so Judy and I decided the only logical choice left for us was to file for bankruptcy. We had moved to a smaller home a few years earlier and somehow were able to keep it out of the bankruptcy filing. We were hoping to keep from losing the house, but to do that I needed to start earning enough money to maintain the monthly mortgage payments. But the prospects for that kept getting slimmer and slimmer.

I gave a lot of thought to starting my own business, even though I didn't have money to buy a business and couldn't start one that required any inventory. I had been on an interview a few months earlier with a company that sold video surveillance equipment to small businesses, and the more I thought about it the more I convinced myself that I could do the same thing. With my technical background I was able to figure out what kind of equipment would be needed, and I didn't have to buy anything until I made a sale. I not only found someone to do the actual installation work, I got my son to work with me doing sales. Loss Reduction Systems was born. All we had to do to keep it alive was go out and find customers. If I had really committed myself to what I was doing I believe that company would have been successful, but I wasn't putting in anywhere near the effort needed to make it happen. In fact, Eric made the company's one and only sale.

I hadn't been putting much effort into anything for quite some time, for all the same reasons as before—no interest, no ability to stay focused, and apparently no real desire to succeed. The one thing I was most aware of was the almost constant feelings of anxiety and helplessness. I was suffering from an acute case of depression but didn't know it. What I did know was that pain and misery had become a part of my daily life, and it was driving me crazy. I had to find a way to stop it, but no matter what I tried I couldn't make the constant stomach aches, headaches, and body aches go away. I was taking medication but it either helped for only a few minutes at a time or not at all. And to make matters worse, I was getting very little sleep. On a good night I might get a total of two or three hours, but the most in any one stretch was about twenty minutes. I went to bed tired, got out of bed tired, and my ass dragged all day.

In addition to my suffering, it was evident that Judy was suffering as well. I knew she was angry and frustrated with me and my inability to provide financial stability for our family. There seemed to be only one way out of my despair, and to provide some financial security for Judy at the same time. I had a $100,000 life insurance policy, and after verifying that it would pay off for death by suicide, I made up my mind. I drove to a liquor store and bought a pint of cheap whiskey, stopped at a 7-11 for a pack of Marlboroughs, and then parked in a secluded area of a nearby park. After writing a goodbye letter to Judy and my children, I lit a cigarette—my first in over ten years—and washed down a handful of prescription pills with the whiskey. I remember finishing the cigarette, tossing it out the window, and lighting a second one, but nothing after that. Everything went dark and my mind went blank. There were no thoughts, no dreams, no tunnels, no bright light, and no relatives waiting to greet me. There was absolutely nothing. Is that what death really is, emptiness, nonexistence, oblivion? Or was it that way for me because I didn't die, because it wasn't my time? More questions with no answers.

I was later told that a woman walking through the park saw me slumped over the steering wheel and called 9-1-1. I was taken by ambulance to the closest hospital, where they pumped my stomach, kept me sedated, then put me in the psych ward, where I woke up a few days later. At first I didn't know where I was or even who I was.

I was confused; my mind was filled with thoughts that made no sense. A woman I didn't recognize was standing next to the bed holding my hand, and a nurse was moving around the room. As my mind began to clear I saw it was Judy holding my hand, and slowly things started to come back to me. My first thoughts were that I couldn't even succeed at killing myself. My suicide attempt had failed, just as my career had. I was a failure at life and a failure at death. I was doomed to a life of pain and suffering, and I couldn't figure out why. Years later, a fellow Vietnam veteran said to me "Howard, Vietnam couldn't kill me, the streets couldn't kill me, and I couldn't even kill myself. God must have a pretty warped sense of humor or he just really loves to fuck around with me." Thinking back, I remember having almost identical thoughts lying in that hospital bed.

The hospital psychiatrist wanted to keep me for 30 days of observation and therapy, and I just wanted to get the hell out of there as quickly as possible. Somehow I managed to convince him that I knew my suicide attempt was a big mistake and that I was mentally stable. He finally agreed to discharge me after a week, but only with the stipulation that I first make arrangements to get therapy from a private psychologist. I scheduled an appointment with a female therapist through a Family Services group and did meet with her regularly for a few months. During all that time there was no discussion of the possibility my military service might have contributed to my depressed mental state. She never even asked whether I had been in the military, and I never thought to mention it, even though I still had regular episodes of nightmares and flashbacks.

As the psychologist didn't seem to be helping me, I eventually stopped seeing her and made another attempt at working. I interviewed with the sales manager of a small independent insurance agency to sell supplemental Medicare insurance. I hit it off well with him in spite of my poor work history and he offered me the job, which I readily took. We actually remained friends well after we were both gone from the company. The company provided me with training and assistance to get licensed with the state to sell both life and health insurance. I did my best to concentrate on the job, and for a while I was able to stay focused. In fact, I was doing fairly well considering insurance sales was totally new to me. But before I knew it I was losing interest and motivation once again. I was right back where I had been before my breakdown. Instead of going to work, I often went to a park that overlooked the Delaware River. I would get out of the car and just stare at the water and the occasional boat going by, or just stay in the car and stare into space. And thoughts of suicide resurfaced.

In 1992, my son decided he wanted to open his own retail business, and in early '93 he opened a coffee shop in downtown Philadelphia. He somehow convinced both Judy and me to help him until he could afford to hire employees. Judy worked with him weekdays and I did on weekends. I was still going through the motions of selling insurance during the week but with no real interest in it and with no success at all. I struggled with it as best I could but it just wasn't working, so I finally gave up trying. Eric's business was off to a good start and if it wasn't for him, I probably would not be alive today. He not only put me to work in his coffee shop, he rented an apartment for the three of us when our house eventually got repossessed. Judy had been getting a very small salary which wasn't quite enough for the two of us to live on, so Eric paid for our living expenses and insurance coverage. And even though there were many times when I did or said things that surely would have gotten me immediately fired by any other employer, Eric continued to put up with me. It didn't cure my depression, although having a place to go each day instead of sitting around the house did help. Yet through it all, the nightmares, flashbacks, and panic attacks continued to haunt me on a regular basis, as did the thoughts of another attempt at suicide.

Chapter 18 - PTSD

One afternoon a man I had not seen before came into the shop for a cup of coffee. As he took out money to pay I saw his money clip had a First Cavalry insignia on it. I told him I had been in the Cav and we spent a few minutes exchanging information about where and when we served. Both of us had been grunts in Vietnam at the same time, I was with the 1st of the 5th and he was with the 2nd of the 5th. He told me his name was Fred Sammartino, that he lived in New Jersey, and had some type of government job.

Fred began coming in regularly, and on one occasion he told me he had applied for disability compensation from the VA. I asked him what for and he wrote down four letters on a piece of paper—P-T-S-D. I had no idea what the letters meant. When he said they stood for post traumatic stress disorder, I still had no idea what it was. When he explained it was similar to shell shock or battle fatigue, I finally had some sense of what he was talking about. However, it didn't register with me that someone could get disability compensation for something like that, especially twenty or more years after the fact. He said as far as he was concerned every Vietnam veteran who went through as much shit as we did with the First Cav should be entitled to it. He talked more about it every time he came in the store, saying guys like us should be approved automatically. But, of course, that wasn't the way the VA worked. In addition to all the paperwork he had to submit, there was an extensive evaluation process that he had to undergo, and then it would take a while before being notified of the results. In the meantime, he was in therapy for post-traumatic stress at the Camden County (New Jersey) Vet Center, and he urged me to do the same. As he learned more about my life after Vietnam, the more he kept telling me that he believed I was suffering from the disorder. All along it sounded like the whole PTSD thing was some kind of a scam that enabled guys to take advantage of the system. But I was curious about it, and I did have issues that could have been Vietnam related, so a few days later I called the Vet Center and made an appointment to see a counselor.

Congress established the Vet Center Program as part of the VA system in 1979 out of a long-overdue recognition that a significant number of Vietnam veterans were still experiencing serious readjustment problems. It consists of community-based centers to provide a broad range of counseling, outreach, and referral services to help eligible veterans make a satisfying post-war readjustment to civilian life. Unlike the VA hospitals that provide medical treatment for both physical and mental issues, the Vet Center's mission is primarily to help veterans with PTSD and related readjustment problems. They are staffed by psychologists and mental health therapists and counselors, and they refer veterans with other needs to the appropriate VA departments or facilities.

My first meeting at the Camden County Vet Center was with the director, Norm Sooy. He said because I lived in Philadelphia I should probably go the Vet Center there, but because I was already in his office he had me talk to one of his counselors, Bob Burrell.

Bob was also a Vietnam veteran and had been a grunt like me, but with the Marines. He had been diagnosed with PTSD a number of years before, and benefited so much from the help he received from the Vet Center program he decided to become a counselor himself to help other vets with similar readjustment issues. During that first meeting he asked me a lot of questions about my tour in Vietnam. The easy ones were my rank, MOS, and what unit I was with. He followed that up with a few questions about irritability, anger, and anxiety. They weren't too difficult to talk about, but then he asked about my nightmares and flashbacks; whether any of them were recurring, and if I could describe them in detail. That was the tough part. I did indeed have dreams and flashbacks about some of my combat experiences, but these were things I had never talked about—not with Judy, not with friends, not with anyone. —and I didn't want to talk about them with Bob. Three of my Vietnam experiences did repeat with regularity: Sergeant Smith's dead body swinging in the trees, my face-to-face encounter with the NVA point man, and getting shot down in the Psyops helicopter. I did tell Bob there were a few recurring dreams and flashbacks that bothered me, but that was as far as I was able to go. I couldn't bring myself to go into any details. In fact, just thinking about them brought on a panic attack. When I finally calmed down he began telling me about some of his combat experiences, which I knew right away was an attempt to get me comfortable enough to open up about mine. That did put me a little more at ease with him, but it wasn't enough to get me talking. I was afraid doing so would make me feel even worse.

Bob said he understood and didn't push it any further. He handed me a sheet of paper listing the classic symptoms of combat PTSD, and asked if I could relate to any of them. The farther down the list I got the more perplexed I became. Before seeing the list I expected to match up with a few of the symptoms, but not to almost all of them. Yet, there were only a couple that did not hit home. Here is the list he showed me:

Distressing recollections

Flashbacks (feeling as if you're back in combat while awake)

Nightmares (frequent recurrent combat images while asleep)

Survivor Guilt

Feeling anxious or fearful (as if you're back in the combat zone again)

Extensive and active avoidance of people, especially crowds

Loss of interest

Feeling detached from others

Feeling disconnected from the world around you and things that happen to you

Restricting your emotions

Shutting down (feeling emotionally and/or physically numb)

Trouble remembering important parts of what happened during traumatic events

Things around you seem strange or unreal

Feeling strange and/or experiencing weird physical sensations

Not feeling pain or other sensations

Difficulty sleeping

Irritability

Outbursts of anger

Difficulty concentrating or thinking clearly

An exaggerated startle response (triggers bring you back to a certain combat zone event)

Being in a state of hyper-vigilance (feeling the need to always be prepared for danger)

Being overly angry or aggressive

Experiencing panic attacks

When I finished looking over the list we talked about PTSD—what it is, and the effects it can have on those who suffer from it. He went on to explain that it's a chronic anxiety disorder, and while there is no cure, there are effective treatments that can help lessen the symptoms. Some vets respond well to various anti-depressants and anti-anxiety medications, others to psychological therapy, and still others to some combination of both methods. He didn't want to overwhelm me any more than he already had, so he said we would discuss all these things in more detail during our next meeting.

I left Bob's office with three things: the symptom list, a follow-up appointment with him for the following week, and an appointment with Bob O'Hara, the office VSO (Veteran Service Officer) to start working on a disability claim with the VA. All the way home my mind was in a jumble of confusion and I didn't know exactly what to make of it. I thought I had gone there more out of curiosity than anything else, but maybe subconsciously I went because I was looking for answers and hoped to find them there. It was obvious I had problems, and I suspected my tour in Vietnam could have played a role, but I certainly didn't think all of my issues were caused by Vietnam. I kept going over the symptom list in my mind and the more I did the more disturbed I became. Did I really have PTSD, and if so, what exactly did that mean? What type of treatment would I get and would it actually help? PTSD is a mental disorder, so did that mean I was crazy? Would I get put away in some institution somewhere? More questions, but this time maybe I could actually find some answers.

As soon as I got home I went straight to the computer and started researching combat PTSD. The more I read the more sense it began to make. When Judy came home late that afternoon I was still sitting in front of the computer with a pile of information on PTSD that I had printed. I showed her the list Bob had given me and told her it's very likely I had the condition. We talked about the things on the list that she could immediately associate with me, and some of the things that were not so obvious. Things like the extent of dreams and flashbacks I was having, my survivor guilt, my inability to stay focused and concentrate, and my constant feelings of anxiety. I knew she too wasn't sure about it at first, but the more we discussed it, the more she realized that many of my actions and my attitude toward people did match up with the symptom list. It took some time for this new revelation to sink in for both of us, but when we finally accepted the fact that it was a mental condition causing my problems, it literally saved our marriage. I didn't realize that Judy had been just one step away from throwing in the towel and filing for divorce. To say she was fed up with me is an understatement. Trying to deal with our financial woes, losing our house, and my erratic behavior had taken an enormous toll on her. She was at the end of her rope. But the realization that PTSD was the probable cause of it all, that I really had very little control over my life, and that there was treatment available, brought us closer together than we had been in many years.

When I met with Bob O'Hara, I mentioned the previous disability rating I had for my ankle, and he helped me file the paperwork to re-establish the original rating for it. That was pretty straightforward, but providing sufficient documentation to support a PTSD disability claim was much more involved. We discussed what I needed to accompany the application, and once I had it all together he would help me with the submission. The completed application was submitted about two weeks later. He said I would get acknowledgements from the VA once they received my paperwork, and that would be followed by separate C & P (Compensation and Pension) examinations for the two claims. Some time after that, probably many months, I would receive decision letters for each claim. The VA disability claim processes followed the traditional military policy of *hurry up and wait*, and it was not uncommon for the entire process to run into years.

Once that was done I had my follow-up meeting with Bob Burrell. We discussed my starting regular therapy sessions. In his opinion, the Vet Center program provided the most effective treatment for combat PTSD. He also recommended going to the

Philadelphia VA Hospital and enrolling in the VA Health System. I could then request an evaluation with one of the psychiatrists in the mental health clinic who could prescribe medication to help ease my depression and anxiety while I underwent therapy. He also thought I would be better off going to the downtown Philadelphia Vet Center instead of staying with the Camden facility, primarily because it would be more convenient. It was located a short bus ride from my apartment, and close enough that I could even walk there. The therapist he recommended was Art Diaz, an Air Force veteran who had a lot of experience and success dealing with PTSD sufferers. It did make sense to go to the closer center, so I never got into any further discussions with Bob. I stopped at the Philly center a few days later and set up an appointment with Art. And although I had some very rough sessions with him over the years, even stopping therapy with him for a time, he played a major role in helping me. I never saw Bob Burrell again, and less than a year later I found out he had died of cancer, most likely caused by exposure to Agent Orange, the chemical agent used extensively to defoliate dense forest areas in Vietnam.

During my first session with Art he gave me a rundown of his background and his overall experience treating men with post traumatic stress issues, not only combat veterans, but police officers and fire-fighters as well. Like Bob, he started off by asking basic questions about my army service before getting into the specifics of my Vietnam experiences. He explained that the most important aspect of the therapy was to get me to openly discuss the most traumatic events I could remember. I wasn't too happy about that, but I had read where that seemed to be the most effective treatment method. I told him how uncomfortable I felt about it, and he said he wouldn't rush me into anything until he was sure I was ready for it, he would take it very slow and easy. He also agreed with Bob about enrolling in the VA health system, not only to get medications to help me deal with my PTSD, but also to have access to the whole range of medical services available there.

I went to the VA hospital, filled out the required paperwork, and was pleasantly surprised that my enrollment didn't take as long as I thought it might. I was scheduled for a complete physical, and the doctor who examined me became my primary care doctor. I was also given an appointment for a psychological evaluation at the hospital's mental health clinic. I did meet with one of the staff psychiatrists, but it wasn't without complications. I arrived on time, had a short wait before being ushered into what looked like an interrogation room on a TV cop show, and after a much longer wait a young female psychiatric intern finally came in. She was there to do a preliminary evaluation and was equipped with a questionnaire, a pencil, limited information about me, and a very sour attitude. After a brief introduction she jumped right into the questionnaire, most of which seemed completely unrelated to my reason for being there. I answered the questions as best I could, but when they began probing my Vietnam experiences I wasn't able to provide answers that satisfied her. In fact, she became very annoyed with me, which in turn got me pissed off at her. I asked if she had any experience dealing with combat vets suffering from PTSD. She said no, but added that it shouldn't matter one way or the other. Well, it damned sure did matter to me and I let her know exactly how much—very loudly and with a lot of anger in my voice. Apparently my outburst frightened her enough to hastily leave the room, saying someone else would be in to take her place. I figured it would be one of the hospital police officers to throw me out, but instead it was a 60-ish man with a straggly beard and a pony tail, who introduced himself as the head of the mental health department. He calmed me down, apologized for the inexperienced intern who upset me, discussed my situation without using a canned questionnaire, and then made a follow-up appointment for me with the psychiatrist he was assigning me to.

A week later I met with the psychiatrist. His job was primarily to prescribe appropriate medications, and if therapy was needed he would have a staff psychologist handle that part of the treatment process. He prescribed anti-depressant and anti-anxiety medications, and scheduled me for a series of monthly follow-up appointments to monitor my progress and to adjust my medications as needed. He did have me meet with one of the psychologists, who said there was no need to continue with him as I had already started therapy at the Vet Center. Seeing two different therapists for the same issue could create more problems than it solved.

Chapter 19 – VA Disability

As my weekly therapy sessions at the Vet Center continued, not only did I learn much more about PTSD, Judy did as well. In addition to the material I passed along to her, she got a lot of helpful information by attending a number of group sessions at the VA hospital that were specifically geared to spouses of vets with PTSD. She gained more knowledge about what I was going through, and meeting other wives with similar issues enabled her to better handle the whole situation. Even though she was able to understand why I got angry over little things and often directed my anger at her, having to deal with those things on a constant basis wasn't easy. She deserves a lot of credit for having the perseverance and determination to put up with all my crap for so many years. In fact, after saying almost those exact words to Art one day, I added that she deserved a medal for all the suffering I had put her through. He listened intently and then asked why I hadn't given her one yet. The very next day I ordered a Purple Heart medal and wrote a poem to accompany it. I had never written a poem in my life and didn't know where to start, but as I sat down in front of my computer the right words just came to me. The poem basically told her she was being awarded the medal because of the psychological wounds I had inflicted on her as a byproduct of my PTSD. (A copy of it is in the Addendum at the end of the book).

Surprisingly, it didn't take long for the VA to schedule the two C & P exams—the first being for my ankle. The orthopedic doctor had x-rays taken and did a thorough examination, which resulted in my ten-percent service-related disability rating being restored. It was retroactive to the date of my recent claim submission, unfortunately not from when it stopped all those many years before, but I wasn't complaining. What I did complain about was the psychological exam I went through for the PTSD claim and the psychiatrist who did the evaluation. He was Asian, which in itself was not a problem, but his very heavy accent was. It made him almost impossible to understand, and his poor use of the English language didn't help matters. Just about every question he asked had to be repeated, often two or three times. I was getting frustrated and it became difficult to keep my anger under control. I even came close to walking out, but I knew that would only work against me, so I somehow forced myself to stick with it. The other issue I had was his repeated questions about drug and alcohol use. I assured him I was not on drugs of any kind and only drank socially, but every other question touched on drug use and alcohol consumption. He kept insisting it wasn't possible to have PTSD without some drug or alcohol abuse. That made me feel like I was wasting my time, unless I admitted to being a junkie or an alcoholic, but I wasn't going to lie to him, or anyone else, even if it resulted in my claim being denied.

When I finally received the decision letter, which was almost totally based on that exam, I was shocked to see I was approved for a 50-percent service-connected disability rating. I would be getting a check retroactive to the date of my application submission, and regular disability checks would follow on the first of each month. I contacted Bob O'Hara and told him about the rating. He was happy for me, but thought it should have been higher, and urged me to file an appeal. He suggested I get in touch with a certain VSO he knew from the VFW (Veterans of Foreign Wars) regional office who had good results with disability appeals. I did just that and met with the man Bob recommended a week later. He helped me submit an appeal requesting a re-evaluation of my claim. His only concern about getting the rating upgraded was the psychiatrist who evaluated me. Despite his language issues, he had a pretty good track record and his recommendations were rarely overturned. But in spite of that, he did not agree with the psychiatrist's comments about drugs and alcohol use. He said my mental health history and condition, my therapy report from Art Diaz, and my combat experiences gave me a reasonable chance of getting my rating upgraded.

When it came time to present my case to the reviewer, the VSO was there with me, acting on my behalf in the same way a lawyer would. And he did a superb job. My rating was increased to 100-percent and it was made retroactive to my initial filing date. The fixed monthly income I would be receiving gave me a sense of financial security I hadn't had in a very long time. Judy was still working in the coffee shop and getting a small salary, plus Eric was still taking care of the apartment rent and health insurance. I tried to help out in the shop as best I could, but I usually was more of a burden than a help, so my involvement was very limited. The disability payments really took a lot of pressure off of us.

My therapy sessions with Art certainly enabled me to understand more about PTSD and why it affected me the way it did, but that didn't improve my ability to handle my issues any better. In fact, I had gotten pretty frustrated with the whole psychotherapy routine. There were a few times when I felt I was benefiting from it, but overall it seemed like every one step forward resulted in one or two steps backward. When discussing some of my outward symptoms of PTSD, such as anger, I listened to Art's suggestions about recognizing the triggers and how to use that insight to minimize my anger outbursts. I would sit in his office and agree that the steps he said to follow made sense, but when faced with an actual situation, those recommendations never entered my mind. The anger took control before I had a chance to follow Art's recommended plan of action. To make matters worse, when I did get angry, even over something dumb or pointless, it often took me days to calm down. And it was like that with almost everything we worked on. His suggestions made perfect sense in his office, but when I needed to implement one of them I wasn't able to make it happen. I seemed to be going nowhere fast.

My other problem with the therapy was that many sessions seemed to intensify my issues instead of minimizing them. Instead of improving, I was doing the reverse. Much of the therapy was centered on having me relive my most traumatic events. But the more I talked about those previously buried memories, the more details I began to remember, and the more I was plagued with nightmares, flashbacks, and higher anxiety. Panic attacks were occurring with more intensity and regularity, and it took days for the anxiety to ease up after the sessions. Most nights before scheduled therapy sessions were spent worrying about what new memories would come to light and any setbacks they might generate. The next mornings would usually start off in the bathroom with a bout of diarrhea.

To find a more successful treatment approach, Art tried what was then a relatively new procedure called Eye Movement Desensitization and Reprocessing, or EMDR. He would move his finger back and forth in front of my face as I recalled a traumatic event, and I had to keep following his hand motions with just my eyes. Art didn't go into a detailed explanation of exactly how the procedure worked; he just said other VA therapists were using it with success. Unfortunately, EMDR left me in an even worse state than the traditional methods he had used. My anxiety already was high before the sessions, but with EMDR it was off the scale by the time the session ended. And it took even longer for my anxiety level to come down. When it finally did subside, it was time for another session and the whole cycle started over again. I felt like I was on a constant roller coaster ride with no way to get off of it. I couldn't continue that way, so I pulled the plug and stopped my therapy sessions completely.

I also stopped seeing my psychiatrist, but for a different reason: the side effects to every drug he prescribed. Sometimes it was a bad case of diarrhea or stomach cramps, other times sluggishness so extreme I could hardly function. And a number of times the medicines actually increased the problems they were intended to improve, especially my anxiety. When I told him the most recent drug he prescribed put me in a state of constant agitation, he said I shouldn't be concerned—he had dozens more he could try until he found one that worked. By that time he already had tried about a dozen different ones and there was no way I could continue putting myself through the misery of their side effects. The anti-depressants had left me more depressed than ever. I had all I could take and I told him so, and that was my last session with him.

I did, however, continue seeing my primary care doctor for general medical care, so I did go to the VA hospital on somewhat of a regular basis. It was on one of those hospital visits that I ran into Fred Sammartino. It had been a while since we had seen each other, so we spent some time catching up. He had moved to somewhere in New England, but recently came back to New Jersey. When I brought him up to date on my disability status he said he knew all about it—that he had been keeping tabs on me. That seemed a bit odd, but before I had a chance to question him on it he said he was late for an appointment, and he took off.

Chapter 20 – Group Therapy

I was off the meds and through with therapy, but my problems were still there. I had learned much more about what my PTSD issues were and how they affected me, but no matter how much more I read on my own, it wasn't enough to get them resolved. I was in a state of limbo. My finances had improved considerably thanks to the monthly VA disability income, which certainly had a positive effect on my life, but that wasn't enough either. So after more than a year of no therapy, I figured maybe the time was right to try again. I was still gun-shy about going back to Art at the Vet Center, so I went to the VA hospital and scheduled an appointment with the psychologist I had seen before. It took only a few sessions for him to conclude that my depression had worsened since he last saw me, and he was understandably concerned.

He wanted me to go to the Coatesville, Pennsylvania VA Hospital for its six-week in-patient PTSD program. He felt that treatment program would be the best way for me to get the help I needed. I, however, didn't react well to the thought of being hospitalized for just six days, let alone six weeks. He was convinced Coatesville was the only way I could get treatment that would really improve my condition, and I was convinced that hospitalized treatment would not work for me. After we went back and forth about it, he offered me one possible alternative—group therapy. He had seen cases where group sessions worked when individual therapy failed. The down side, however, was the location and the group leader. The only active group in the area with room for an additional participant was at the Philly Vet Center, and Art Diaz was the therapist running it. Considering my previous hang-ups with Art, I wasn't at all pleased about that. But as it was the only way to avoid the Coatesville route, other than continue to do without any therapy, I agreed to give it a try. The one stipulation was that I had to consent to entering the Coatesville program if the group therapy didn't work out, which I reluctantly agreed to.

After Art was contacted and understood the situation, I met with him for a few individual sessions so he could get up to speed on my current condition and evaluate whether he thought group therapy would work for me. He was uncertain about it, but agreed that it would be worth trying, and I would still have to meet with him individually on a regular basis for him to monitor my progress.

There were nine guys present at my first group session, all of who had been meeting together for some time. Art had me introduce myself, give the guys some general background on my military service, tell them how I came to be in the group, and then talk about some of the traumatic events I had experienced in 'Nam. Everything was okay until I hit the last part. I had discussed some of those things with Art in private sessions, which was tough enough, but never in front of a group, especially a bunch of guys I didn't know and didn't feel comfortable with. As time went on, however, I was slowly able to overcome my reluctance to talk about my experiences. I became more relaxed with the guys, especially once I realized how much we all had in common. Not only had we experienced similar traumatic events in 'Nam, we were all dealing with many of the very same PTSD issues. That commonality of past experiences and present issues made me recognize for the first time since Vietnam that there were other men I could talk to freely, men who could truly understand what I was going through and vice versa. That mutual understanding is what helped develop a bond between us almost as strong as if we had actually fought side by side in combat. It was exactly what I needed and it enabled me to deal with my issues better than any previous treatment. There still were times when discussions brought up painful memories, especially when a new member came into the group and mentioned helicopters. The first time it happened, I had a flashback of when I got shot down when the guy began talking about his experiences as a door gunner. At the very next session, I had a pretty severe panic attack as soon as that same guy walked into the room. But those situations eventually became much less frequent and easier for me to handle. Art later said that he told new guys coming into the group not to talk about helicopters until he felt I was better equipped to deal with it.

There were times when I mentioned something I was going through and one of the guys would offer advice based on his experience with a similar situation. The fact that it came from a fellow vet who suffered as I did made all the difference in the world. If he had success dealing with that particular issue, I believed that I should be able to as well. And more often than not, I could. A few times I was unable to get to the weekly meeting, and when that happened I felt like something was missing from my life. I couldn't wait for the following week to get together with my new brothers. Joining the group was by far one of the best things that happened to me after being diagnosed with PTSD.

Right from the start I noticed that many of the guys were wearing baseball-type hats with military or veteran insignias on them. For years I wanted to hide my military service from everyone—I didn't want to expose myself to more of the abuse I had experienced. But being with guys who displayed their service in public created a conflict for me. I discussed it with the group, and the more we talked about it, the more I came to accept the idea that I had absolutely nothing to be ashamed of or embarrassed about. I was proud that I had served my country, and I realized I should not be afraid to openly show that pride. I had a cap with an American flag on it and I added a small First Cavalry pin to it. Slowly, I built up to wearing one with a First Cav patch sewn on it, and then to one that actually said Vietnam Veteran. I now have about a dozen different hats, including a First Cav Stetson, with an assortment of patches and pins that I wear regularly. I am proud of my service and now display that pride every chance I get. And if some people are turned off by what they see, that's on them, not me. So far, I've had no negative comments. In fact, just the opposite—many people have actually shook my hand and thanked me for my service.

There was another experience with the group that was very instrumental in helping me deal with an issue that had bothered me for some time. For many years, my inability to remember the names of the guys from Echo Recon who died in action ate away at me.

Even Sergeant Smith's name eluded me for a very long time. When Art arranged a bus trip to the Vietnam Memorial Wall in Washington I was hesitant about going. My only contact with the Wall was when Judy and I were in D.C. for our 25th wedding anniversary and just happened to stumble onto it. I wasn't prepared for it, and it wasn't a good experience. So when I was faced with returning, I wasn't sure if I could handle it. The group convinced me that it might be good therapy and if I didn't react well I could always walk around other areas of Washington or just stay on the bus. It wasn't easy walking down the long walkway that goes from one end of the Wall to the other, but I did it. I thought I could do it quickly and without looking at the names, but once I glanced at the first panel I was mesmerized. The names are in chronological order, according to the date of death, and within each day, they are alphabetized. I stopped at most of the panels, but not those that listed the names from my time in Vietnam. That was more than I was able to handle. But I did go back to the Wall a few more times and finally got up the courage to look at those panels too. Eventually I did remember the names that had eluded me for so long, and that gave me some degree of closure.

The other bus trip Art arranged was to the National Archives that houses documents from the Vietnam War era. It's on the grounds of the University of Maryland. Those of us who planned to go on the trip submitted a request for the after-action reports from our respective units during specified times, and those documents were waiting for us when we got there. The reports I reviewed were the written accounts of the daily activities of all the companies in the First Cav's Second Brigade, including the communications between Echo Recon and our company command. Most of them had been typed from the original handwritten reports, but some were the actual handwritten originals, in different writing styles and ink colors—complete with smeared dirt and blood stains. Seeing the dried blood freaked me out so much I had to get away from it for a while. Soaking my face with cold water in the men's room helped, but I was nervous about going back to the reports. I was afraid they might stir up still-buried memories that might undo some of the positive results I had gained from therapy. But I forced myself to go back to them and I'm glad I did. While more recollections did result from reading more of the reports, some of my earlier memories that had been jumbled together became untangled and made more sense to me. And that actually turned out to be much more of a positive than a negative.

Among the many side benefits of being in the group, one actually helped Judy more than me. The majority of the guys were not married, yet most had been through multiple marriages and divorces. A few, however, had wives who had hung in there with them over the years, just as Judy had with me. I became very friendly with one guy in particular, which led to our wives also developing a strong friendship. The two women talked a lot about their common issues related to our PTSD, how it affected them, and how they handled it. They benefited in almost the same way I did from the group.

In December of 1998, two years after receiving my 100-percent disability, I underwent a required follow-up review to determine if my rating was to be continued. The exam lasted over an hour, during which I was asked a barrage of questions designed to help the examiner assess my current mental state and how I was dealing with my PTSD issues. Based on the comments she made afterwards, I was fairly certain the outcome would not only be a continuation of my 100-percent disability status, but that it would be reclassified to T & P (Total and Permanent). Four months later I received a letter advising me of the results of that review, and I was floored. Here is exactly how the letter began:

We have denied your claim for service-connected disability compensation. In reaching this decision we considered the following evidence:

VA examination date December 7, 1998
The enclosed Rating Decision provides a summary of the evidence we considered in making this decision, and the reasons and basis of our determination.

I couldn't believe my eyes. I was stunned—no, I was devastated. I kept asking myself how this could happen. Everything was finally going well—my life had been steadily improving. What the hell would happen to me now? Anger was building up, and I felt like I wanted to punch somebody out, and probably would have if anyone had been in the room with me. I sat down, totally drained, and just as I was about to tear the letter to shreds, the blue sheet of paper with the Decision Summary caught my eye. I stopped and looked at it, and it's a damn good thing I did. Here's how that page began:

ISSUE: Evaluation of post traumatic stress disorder currently evaluated at 100% disabling.

EVIDENCE: VA examination dated December 7, 1998

DECISION: Post traumatic stress disorder, which is currently 100% disabling, is continued.

The rest of the decision page gave a review of the examination and ended with this line:

No future examinations will be scheduled because this condition is now considered permanent.

In the span of a few minutes I had gone from having positive expectations, to utter devastation, to sheer relief. I had no idea why the opening paragraph was worded to imply a denial of my disability rating. I sat there wondering why bureaucratic agencies do such things, but I finally told myself as long as my 100-percent status was continuing permanently it really didn't matter.

Many additional benefits become available with a total and permanent 100-percent rating. Two of the most important ones are the tax-free income I receive for life and the free medical care I get at any VA hospital or clinic. Not only do I get all of my medical treatments, I also get complete dental work, eye exams and glasses, and all of my medications at no cost. In addition, Judy became eligible for the ChampVA program, which paid 75-percent of her medical and hospital bills, and 100-percent of her mail-in prescriptions, with only a $50 annual deductible. That was before she was on Medicare, and now that she is on Medicare, ChampVA has become her Medicare Supplement and still pays for all of her medications. In addition, I pay no real estate taxes—a state benefit—and have access to most military facilities, including base lodging and commissary privileges, as well as a variety of other military discounts. And even a 70 to 90-percent rating can provide all the benefits of a 100-percent rating. A separate application must be submitted for *Individual Unemployability*, and if approved, the vet will receive the same benefits and monthly disability payments that he would get if the rating was 100-percent.

One of the other side benefits of being in group therapy was the information we got from one another, especially regarding benefits we may not have been aware of. I heard from some of the guys in my group that once a VA disability rating of 100-percent is classified as permanent, we could apply for Social Security disability. There is no automatic approval, which means going through a pretty tough evaluation process by Social Security, even though the VA's 100-percent disability rating indicates total unemployability. A person's obvious physical impairments will generally support his or her claim of being unable to work, but with PTSD there are no such visual indicators to support a disability claim. And despite being classified by the VA as unemployable, mental health professionals contracted by Social Security have to independently arrive at that same conclusion.

Chapter 21 – SSD

Shortly after I received my 100-percent T & P rating I submitted an application for Social Security Disability. I filled out the required forms at my local Social Security office, and after a long wait I was scheduled for a psychological evaluation exam with a private Philadelphia psychiatrist. I arrived about ten minutes early but had to wait almost an hour before I was seen. The exam lasted all of 15 minutes, most of which was spent listening to him tell me what made him such a terrific psychiatrist. He was on the staff of the University of Pennsylvania Hospital, taught at Penn's medical school, and had written numerous papers on a variety of mental health issues. He then asked me to answer a few ridiculous questions: Who was the mayor of Philadelphia? Who was the President of the United States? What was that day's date? Would I count backward from 100, by 3s? He stopped me when I correctly reached 85, and that was the end of the exam. As he ushered me out of the office, he said I would receive a letter indicating whether my application was approved.

I was so infuriated I immediately wrote a letter to the Social Security Administration detailing my so-called exam. About a month later I was surprised to receive a letter of apology, along with appointment information for an exam with a different evaluator, this time a woman psychologist. The first thing I did when I got there was to ask her what her credentials were and if she had experience with combat PTSD patients. She said her PTSD experience was limited to a few rape victims, and she had zero experience with military veterans. When I asked her how she could possibly do an effective evaluation, she got very defensive and asked if I wanted to terminate the session. I knew if I did my claim would be rejected, so I gave in and stayed for an hour of questions that once again made little sense to me. And, of course, the letter I received from Social Security was a denial of disability benefits. It said the two exam reports indicated that my issues were not severe enough to prevent me from working in some capacity to at least meet the minimum earnings level. At the time, if an applicant was able to earn at least $500 a month he or she was not eligible to receive Social Security Disability benefits. That was quite a ridiculously low threshold, but the only way around it was to prove to them that I was totally unemployable for any and all types of jobs.

I challenged the ruling and eventually was scheduled for an appointment with another Social Security psychologist. This one fell into a category somewhere between the two I had already seen. He said he had some experience with PTSD and gave me what I felt was a reasonable exam, but the results were the same, another denial letter. A few people I talked to said it was fairly common to repeatedly get turned down for PTSD unless you hire a lawyer to help with the claim. One of the guys in my group had also been turned down a few times, but after hiring a law firm to represent him, he was approved. I contacted the firm's he used and with their help another appeal was submitted. This time I was scheduled for a judicial hearing where a judge would listen to arguments for my claim.

About a month before that hearing I ran into Fred again at the hospital. When I told him about my experiences with Social Security he again said he knew all about it, and that I shouldn't be concerned—I would definitely get approved. And just as he rushed off the previous time we met, he did the same thing this time, again before I had a chance to ask him any questions. That was my last contact with him. Was it coincidence that he showed up right before some very important moments in my life? How could he know what would happen? And why, on both occasions, did he say he had been keeping tabs on me? How could he even do that? And what about going to the Vet Center for treatment—would that have happened if it were not for him?

Just before the hearing, my attorney and I were given copies of my complete Social Security claim file to review. In there were all my psychological evaluation reports. The most outlandish was the one from the first psychiatrist, the guy who spent ten of my fifteen minutes telling me how good he was. He stated that I did have PTSD issues, but they were not serious enough to keep me from working at a job I could handle. The report went on to say the type of job that would fit me best was one in which I had as little contact with people as possible, especially those in a management capacity. He recommended I find a job as a night janitor in a school or office building, with little or no contact with anyone. Even the judge thought that report was ridiculous, which I think had some influence on his decision. My attorney laid out what I thought was a solid case for approval, and then the judge asked me a lot of work-related questions. He didn't say whether I would be approved, only that I would receive notification within 90 days, but some of his closing comments left me with a good feeling. Two months later I got the approval letter. It also stated there would be a re-evaluation after five years, but that never happened. And upon turning 65 my payments would stay the same but my status would change from disability to standard Social Security Retirement. Is Fred my guardian angel? Are such things real? It seems all too coincidental not to be.

Chapter 22 – Where Am I Now?

During the years I was in the therapy group many guys came and went. Some were just not able to adapt to group therapy. Some would look to the group for help and advice to deal with issues they were having, but expecting responses and suggestions that matched how they thought their issues should be handled. We believed if we were anything except completely honest with them we would be doing the guys a disservice, so we didn't pull any punches. We offered what we thought were the best approaches to their situations and some men could not handle it when they didn't hear what they wanted to hear. They were the guys who expected us to agree completely with them, and unfortunately, that usually made it impossible for them to stay in the group.

Then there were the guys who tried to embellish their wartime experiences with exaggerations. It usually didn't take us long to see through their stories, and once they realized we were on to them they never returned to the group. One guy even went so far as to falsify an addendum to his DD-214 discharge papers, stating he was in Special Forces and was awarded a Silver Star, neither of which was even close to being true. It's a damn shame that some people believe they have to go to such extremes just to get some amount of recognition or acceptance by others. I really feel sorry for them, but not for those who outright lie about their military experiences in an attempt to take advantage of the system—to get money and benefits they're not entitled to. I believe guys who do that should be punished as severely as the law allows. And even though their numbers are few, when they are exposed, the media too often makes it seem like all of us on disability for PTSD are taking advantage of the system.

I stayed with the group until it was disbanded in February of 2010. At that time it consisted of eight of us who had been together for at least four years. We knew Art was retiring, but we never had any forewarning that the group would be shut down. The very next time we met after Art's departure we were given the news and a date for our group's last session. We were told that we had received enough therapy to be able to deal with our issues on our own—we no longer needed the Vet Center. Looking back, I don't disagree with the decision, but I do disagree with the way it was presented to us, especially the inflexible and impersonal way in which the remaining sessions were conducted. When anyone attempted to discuss a new or previous PTSD-related issue that he was concerned about, we were told it didn't fit into the newly revised schedule of topics that we had to adhere to. There were no exceptions. If we had questions that didn't fit the session's agenda they went unanswered. Nevertheless, in spite of the way my relationship with the Vet Center ended, I can't say enough about the therapy I received there—it was truly a life-saver for me.

For a while we tried to meet for lunch on a regular basis, but that didn't last long. We needed a place to ourselves where we could openly discuss personal matters and restaurants didn't fit the bill. Each week fewer showed up for lunch, and then it was none. However, something had occurred quite unexpectedly a few years earlier that eased some of the pain of the group breaking up—re-establishing contact with many of my comrades from Echo Recon. I saw a post on a veteran's forum web site from someone trying to find former members of E-1-5 of the First Cavalry Division from 1968. I responded to the post and began communicating with Donald Wilson, one of the guys from my old unit. Sometime after we began emailing each other, he put me in contact with Jeff Duvall, another member of our unit with whom he was also in contact. Jeff lives in Virginia, only about three hours away from me, so we decided to meet at a restaurant midway between us for lunch. It was a very emotional meeting, but well worth the pre-meeting anxiety I had experienced. It was about a 90 minute drive to the restaurant, and at least a half a dozen times I thought about turning around and going home. I was worried that meeting a former comrade face to face would cause more of my buried memories to surface that might result in a step backward in my ability to control my PTSD symptoms. Fortunately I didn't bail out and it turned out to be a very positive meeting. We both brought some of our Vietnam pictures and reminisced about our time together. We continued to get together on a regular basis, and Donald flew in from Kentucky to join us for lunch a few months later. That was even more emotional, but also very rewarding.

That was in the summer of 2007 and it led to an important decision for us—to try locating as many of the former members of our unit as we could find and have a real reunion the following year. In August of 2008, after 40 years, six of us got together in

Washington, D.C. for our first formal reunion. And we've held a reunion every year since, with a few more of our brothers in attendance each time. After that first reunion, Jeff and I developed a web site for Echo Recon—www.echorecon1-5.com—in the hopes it would become a tool to attract more of our comrades to future reunions, which it has done. And my ongoing involvement with the web site has been very good for me—it often keeps me busy and it's given me added purpose. But the most amazing thing that came out of the reunions was the immediate re-bonding that we all experienced. It was as though that 40-year gap had never existed. It was an amazing experience, one that renewed our bond of brotherhood and made us acutely aware we will be brothers forever. Unfortunately, some of the guys we've been in contact with, and even a few who have attended one of our reunions, have broken off further contact. I can only assume that they also have PTSD issues, and their contact with former comrades may have had negative results instead of positive ones.

During the time I spent attending the group therapy sessions, I developed some fairly serious health issues. The first was uncovered as a result of a follow-up CAT scan after a bout of pneumonia. My doctor ordered the scan to make sure the pneumonia had cleared up—which it had—but the scan showed a spot on one of my lungs that raised a possible cancer concern. The pulmonary doctor I saw told me it wasn't very significant, and as long as it didn't get any larger there shouldn't be anything to worry about. Until I had a follow-up scan six months later I was pretty worried about it, and that scan did show a slight increase in the size of the spot. It wasn't much of an increase, but enough for me to see a surgeon to have a biopsy done.

The surgeon reassured me that 99-percent of the time the procedure to get a lung tissue sample for the biopsy was pretty simple. Three little holes in my back to get a tiny video camera, a light, and a small surgical device through were all it would take. No major incisions and no lengthy recuperation time. But there was that a one-in-a-hundred chance the procedure would not work, in which case he would have to make an incision in my back to get to the area of the lung he needed to reach. Of course I was that one-in-a-hundred case, but the good news was the biopsy showed no sign of cancer. The spot on the lung was scar tissue, an indication that I have interstitial lung disease. ILD is a condition in which scar tissue forms for no apparent reason, which can prevent the lungs from functioning properly. In my case, I had no symptoms of lung function problems and future CAT scans have not shown any increase in scaring, so the likelihood of long term lung problems is slim. The surgeon sent samples of my lung tissue to about two dozen hospitals around the country, including some VA hospitals, to see if there was a match between my scaring pattern and those typically associated with ILD. There were none. Although there is no way to know for sure, the doctor felt the scarring was probably a result of Agent Orange exposure. Agent Orange was developed to kill jungle foliage in Vietnam wherever it was sprayed, but with no harm to people or animals. That's what was said, but there never was any testing to support the harmless part of the claim. Agent Orange was later proven to be the cause of many varieties of cancers and other serious medical conditions to those exposed.

My other health issues, all of which developed after my lung surgery, are restless leg syndrome, high blood pressure, psoriatic arthritis—a combination of psoriasis and rheumatoid arthritis. Are any or all of these related to Vietnam? It's possible all of them are a result of Agent Orange exposure. Maybe only some are, or maybe none at all, but it's impossible to know. Of course, there's also the possibility that some of my health issues may have developed as byproducts of my PTSD. There's a good chance the high blood pressure falls into that category, but it really doesn't matter at this point. I receive treatment for all my medical problems at the VA and fortunately none of my ailments are life-threatening. In fact, every time I go to the VA hospital and see so many of my fellow veterans on oxygen, on crutches, in wheelchairs, or with missing limbs, I realize my physical problems are almost non-existent in comparison to what those men face every day of their lives. At many of the VA hospitals around the country there are signs and inscriptions that sum up what I see there in a few simple words:

"The Price of Freedom is Visible Here"

As to my medical treatments, I can't say enough about the care I get at the Philadelphia VA Medical Center. We've all heard stories about sub-par care and medical mistakes at some VA hospitals, but the care I've received has been top notch. I have a regular primary care physician, the same one I've had since entering the VA health system. And he is terrific, as is all the medical staff that treated me over the years. That includes doctors, nurses and a variety of technicians. The only hospital personnel I ever had problems with were a few of the non-medical people I had to deal with before seeing a doctor or nurse. Many of the administrative and clerical personnel have been extremely pleasant and helpful, but some acted as though I was interrupting their coffee breaks or personal phone calls, rather than my presence being the reason they had their jobs. A few times I lost my cool when dealing with people like that, but I eventually realized such behavior would only get me into trouble. So instead of blowing up and creating an ugly scene, I would report it to the hospital's Patient Advocate office. And one time I got great satisfaction in knowing I was instrumental in getting one of those incompetent, uncaring, assholes fired.

So how am I now? Overall, I am good. Not great, and I don't think I'll ever reach that level, but compared to how I used to be, I am doing quite well. My financial situation is stable, and even though medical issues exist for both Judy and me, they do not inhibit us from maintaining a fairly active life. Among the most relevant factors in my life today are the six absolutely wonderful grandchildren that I am so fortunate to have. I've heard it said that having a son and a daughter is a rich man's family, so I guess having a son, daughter, and six of the best grandchildren a man could ask for makes me an especially rich man.

And what about my PTSD, do I still have it? Yes. I do, and I always will, and so does Judy. Hers is a consequence of living with me and it is referred to as Secondary PTSD. From what I understand, it's not uncommon for it to develop in spouses of veterans with PTSD. It is not true PTSD, yet the wife can actually display many of the same symptoms as her husband. It's a result of constant exposure to his symptoms, along with being on the receiving end of his verbal and mental abuse. But for the most part, my PTSD influences my life much less than ever and the same holds true for Judy. While I have learned to deal with the disorder, it still has an effect on me. The dreams, the flashbacks, and the panic attacks still occur, but with much less frequency and severity, and some level of anxiety and hyper-vigilance is always with me. When someone pisses me off over some minor incident it's usually out of my system within hours instead of the days it used to take. I know those I love and care about have gained a much better understanding of me through my writing. They now know PTSD was behind the many questionable things I did: why I sometimes acted wild and crazy, easily lost my temper over the smallest things, frequently isolated myself, and often seemed uninterested in them and insensitive to their needs. Most important, I'm confident they won't hold it against me when some or all of those things occasionally happen again, as I know they surely will.

Epilogue

If you are one of the people, I am hoping my story helps—a combat vet with post-traumatic stress issues or the loved one of a sufferer—the question is where do you go from here? You might be a combat vet having problems readjusting to civilian life but can't quite put a finger on what's behind it, or where to go for help. Maybe you suspect, or even know, you have PTSD but aren't sure what to do about it. Or, maybe you do realize your problems are combat-related but want nothing to do with the VA system. Where do you get the help you need? And, if you're a spouse, how do you help your husband deal with his PTSD issues, and also find ways to deal with the effects they have on you?

If you are the veteran, it's critical you seek help, and the best place for that, in my opinion, is one of the many Vet Centers throughout the country. If there are no Vet Centers close by, a VA hospital or clinic would be the next choice. It's not an easy step to take, and I don't want anyone to think it is. If you're still in the service you may feel that making it known you have post-traumatic stress issues will have a negative effect on your military career. And if you are out of the service, you may feel the same about your civilian job. In either case, even though it's not likely to happen, the reality is that it could affect your job or career. But I firmly believe that not getting help will have a far more damaging effect on the rest of your life, and the lives of your family members.

Based on my experiences and those of many fellow veterans, the most effective therapy for post-traumatic stress is psychotherapy.

Medications are often prescribed, and they can ease some of the symptoms temporarily—the nightmares, flashbacks, anxiety, angry outbursts—but they are not addressing the heart of the problem, PTSD. With successful treatment of the PTSD, these symptoms will get taken care of, and medications can be used effectively during psychotherapy. That's not to say PTSD can be cured by therapy, because as yet it is incurable by any means. Hopefully that will change, but for now, there's a very good chance that treatment by an experienced mental health professional—specifically, one with experience treating combat PTSD— can enable you to deal with the disorder, minimizing many of the outward effects and leading to a more normalized life.

One of the more common excuses vets use to rationalize why they don't seek help is that they had prior dealings with the VA and were unhappy with the outcome. In many cases it was either from the frustration of waiting for what seemed like an eternity for things to happen, or being turned down for something you believed should have been approved. It's completely understandable that you're pissed off—I know; I've been there. But if you can muster the energy to put that behind you, it will be worth it in the long run. Believe me, I know it's difficult, but if you are able to hang in there and put up with the bureaucratic bullshit and crap the VA can throw at you, your determination and perseverance will pay off. It almost seems as though the VA drags its feet for disability claims in the hopes that many vets will not pursue their claims. That may or may not be true, but the bottom line is this: if you have a valid claim for disability compensation, it is worth fighting for it, no matter how long it takes, no matter how much crap you have to endure along the way. Remember, when approved, you will receive a lump sum payment retroactive to the date your claim was filed. That can amount to many thousands of dollars, even if you receive less than a 100-percent rating.

There's another reason why some vets refuse to get into the VA system. They may equate receiving disability compensation with welfare, and they are too proud to take what they perceive to be a handout, regardless of how bad their financial state may be. This is one of the reasons why so many combat veterans are homeless. It's absolutely tragic that veterans comprise the largest percentage of the homeless population in this country. In my opinion, and the opinion of many other combat vets I have met over the years, disability compensation is not a handout at all. It's reimbursement for the pain and suffering our government asked us to endure in support of our flag and country. It doesn't matter if the conflicts in which we were involved were unpopular with the general public. It doesn't matter if we disagreed with the government's reason for getting us into war. What does matter is that we responded when we were called upon to support and defend our country and constitution. And, in doing so, if we became casualties, whether physical, mental, or a combination of both, we deserve all the benefits our government has made available to us. As president Abraham Lincoln so appropriately said in his second Inaugural Address:

"Let us strive to finish the work we are in, to bind up the nation's wounds, *to care for him who shall have borne the battle and for his widow and his orphan*,"

Those words were President Lincoln's affirmation of our government's obligation to care for the soldiers injured during war, and to provide for the families of those who perished on the battlefield. The last phrase of that quote eventually became the permanent motto of the Veterans Administration, and rightly so.

Another reason why some vets have a real hang-up about receiving any compensation from the VA is a guilty conscience. The easiest way to explain this one is to relate what a fellow Vietnam veteran said to me when I tried to talk him into going to the VA for help. He drank too much, never held a job for longer than a year at a time, and was constantly getting into fights and barroom brawls, all a result of PTSD. He had enlisted in the army as soon as he turned eighteen, completed Airborne training, and volunteered to become a Ranger. Even though we became close friends, he would not talk to me about anything he did in 'Nam. I could see how painful it was for him any time Vietnam was mentioned. One day, when I tried again to convince him to apply for VA disability, he looked me right in the eye and said: "Howard, there is absolutely no way in hell I will ever take money for the things I did in Vietnam." And no matter how hard I tried to get him to open up, even a little, or to get help with his issues, it was impossible. I just couldn't break through that wall of guilt he had erected. When he eventually was diagnosed with cirrhosis of the liver and was told he needed a transplant, he finally agreed to get help from the VA. Unfortunately, his change of heart came too late; he died of liver failure less than six months later. His name is not on the Wall, but he was as much a casualty of the Vietnam War as those who died on the battlefield. His name is Wayne McNally, in my opinion a true American patriot, and I think about him almost every day.

In addition, there are literally thousand of veterans troubled by many of the same issues I mentioned when describing my demons; men who know they have problems but can't put a finger on why they have them. Any veteran who has been in combat or directly exposed to the horrors of war has been altered in some way. And those changes may become visible anywhere from days to many years after the traumatic experiences. Although subtle symptoms of my PTSD began to show immediately after I returned from 'Nam, they didn't become severe until more than 15 years later, and it was almost 10 years after that before I was diagnosed and got into a treatment program. Many World War II veterans led pretty normal lives until they saw movies like "Saving Private Ryan," which brought back haunting memories that some of them had suppressed for more than 50 years. You have nothing to lose and everything to gain by getting an evaluation by an experienced professional, and the mental health professionals most qualified to recognize and treat combat PTSD issues are those in the VA system.

Please be aware that the suicide rate among combat veterans (22 every single day) is higher than any other group of people in the United States, primarily because so many vets do not get the help they need. And without that help, they are seldom able to handle the suffering that tears them apart. Suicide can seem to be the only avenue available to escape the torment they're going through. As I wrote, I know that from my own personal experience. Luckily, or as fate would have it, my attempt was not successful, but too many other vets have not been as fortunate. If you are experiencing any suicidal thoughts at all, please don't let them turn into action. Get help, and do it now. Getting help is not a weakness; it takes much more strength than people realize, and having survived combat shows you have that strength. Please take that first step, you won't regret it.

And if you are someone who cares about a combat veteran struggling with post-traumatic stress issues, what can you do? How do you help that person, and do it without making things worse for either or both of you? How do you keep stability in your own life with all the issues facing you? How do you keep from losing your cool every time your loved one does something that aggravates the hell out of you? You have to find a way to keep your anger from getting the best of you while you're being bombarded by those symptoms from him, which may be one of the most difficult things for you to do. It's not easy to refrain from lashing back at your spouse or significant other, but if you do, it's almost certain to provoke him even more, and that can only make matters worse. Sometimes it's better to just walk away and give both of you a little time off to cool down.

When you've cooled off, I recommend that you get as much information as you can about PTSD. I have met a number of wives who know their husbands have serious issues and suspect those issues are a result of wartime experiences, but don't really know more than that. Without some idea of what's at the root of your spouse's problems, there isn't much you can do to help. That's why you have to take it upon yourself to learn as much as you can about post-traumatic stress. The better informed you are, the better equipped you will be to deal with it and help your loved one. In addition to the Internet, which certainly has a wealth of information available, I think the best place to start is at one of the Vet Centers. While their primary mission is to provide readjustment assistance to the veterans, they can be a tremendous resource for you as well. They usually have books and pamphlets that can give you a better understanding of the disorder, give you a sense of what the veteran is going through, and provide you with tools and techniques to better cope with it all. And if there are any other resources, such as group information sessions for spouses, they would be able to provide you with that information as well. If there is a group specifically for loved ones—spouses, significant others, children, siblings—I would strongly urge you to take advantage of it. Based on my wife's positive experience, I believe it may be the single best way of helping you deal with the situation you are in. It's also worth checking with the mental health clinic at the nearest VA Medical Center, as they also run groups for spouses. You can find the link to a listing of all the Vet Centers in the Resource section at the end of the book.

Finally, once again, it's important to keep in mind it may well be the PTSD that causes a veteran to act the way he does. He is not in control, his PTSD is. And without the proper help it's often impossible for him to be in command of himself. Even if he is getting help, it can take quite some time before positive changes start to show. It's very important to reassure him that you truly care for him and your goal is to do whatever you can to see him through this extremely difficult and complicated time in his life. Even though you will never know exactly what he's going through, let him know you do understand what's behind it. If he is not getting help to deal with his condition, the best thing you can do for him is find a way to convince him to get that help. It's not an easy task, and there is no magic wand to automatically make it happen. Even though combat vets with PTSD have a lot in common, they are still unique individuals with very different triggers and reactions. But the fact that you know your veteran better than outsiders, and deeply care for him, is what gives you the best chance of convincing him to get into a treatment program. However, if you are not successful in doing that, I'm not sure there is anything you can do on your own to provide the help he desperately needs. You can let him know how much you support him, and you can certainly make constructive suggestions, but he has to be the one to take positive action. Here is the set of guidelines I received from my Vet Center therapist that

Judy found to be extremely helpful in dealing with me. Hopefully you will find it equally beneficial.

Guidelines for a Family Living with a Combat Veteran

- Don't expect the veteran to behave the same way he did before he went into combat.

- Let the veteran know you understand he has a lot of pain that sooner or later he really needs to talk about.

- Let the veteran know that because you have never been in combat you cannot really know his pain.

- At the same time, you want to make it very clear to him that you are interested in learning as much as you can about his combat experiences.

- Let him know you are as prepared as possible to hear what he is feeling and the kinds of feelings he has about his experiences.

- Let the veteran know you will not judge him because of his feelings or behavior.

- Let him know you accept and understand that combat changes people and causes them to do things they would not normally do in civilian life.

- Under all circumstances, demonstrate to the veteran that you care for him and love him, and you are concerned about his emotional problems.

- Encourage the veteran to seek out a professional therapist to discuss and explore his anger and pain.

- Ask the veteran how you can support his taking responsibility to do this for himself.

- It is important that you let the veteran know very clearly that he must take personal responsibility to learn how to express his anger in a constructive and socially acceptable manner.

I wish you the best of luck and hope you are successful in supporting your veteran and helping him or her deal with PTSD. Be sure to check the Addendum and Resources sections that follow. **And to all my fellow combat vets, WELCOME HOME!**

NOTE: I am very much aware that many female soldiers have spent time in war zones, especially over the past ten years, and they are just as susceptible to developing PTSD as their male counterparts. My use of the words "he" or "him" throughout the book is intended to refer to both men and woman soldiers and veterans.

Addendum

The following poem, written by one of the group therapy veterans from the Philadelphia Vet Center, very eloquently describes what many combat veterans go through:

PTSD

There are so few who understand
Just why I am this way
Because I look just like they do
they don't know what to say

And how do I explain to them
that hell is not one place?
It is a full-blown state of mind
that's always in my face

When I am locked behind my wall
or cringing on the floor
They look at me and say, "Stand up!"
And pound upon my door

"Why can't you be like this?" they ask
"Stand up and be a man!
There is no need to cower there
It's time to take your stand!"

They cannot hear the screams I hear
nor see the broken dreams
They de not know the stench of death
the blood in flowing streams

It's not that I'm afraid, you see
Oh no, I was quite brave
Until the shell hit next to me
and made a yawning grave

Where men lay hiding in the dirt
now all of them are dead
There was no time to say goodbye
our common fear unsaid

So locked within my mind I cry
Reach blindly out for sense
Then wretched fear takes hold of me
my bones become a fence

No matter where I run and hide
I can't escape my mind
Familiar things are threatening
and love appears unkind

So up is down and down is up
and all they do is talk
I'm analyzed and classified,
The drugs - they taste like chalk

This pill to get you up, my friend
this one will bring you down
Our aim of course to make you whole
with both feet on the ground

And with this medication
we plan to set you free

But if it doesn't work just right
we may forgo our fee

Oh HO! We were just kidding you
for all must pay their dues
You'll always need our services
when you have the "blues"

But "blues" would be a Sunday stroll
compared to living hell
There is no pill or recompense
to make these visions well

I tried to drink away the fear
but people shied away
Ashamed by my foul drunkenness
and dreading each new day

If I could make them see my heart
and show them that I care
Explain the demons in my head
would they then treat me fair?

Oh, God in Heaven - where are you?
Please take me by the hand
And drive away the Beast from me
to rise up as a man

Let me march and not grow weary
go forth into the sun
Be loved and fully understood
until my race is run.

The following is my poem to Judy that accompanied the medal I gave her:

You Deserve a Medal

Less than a year from the
day we were wed,
a draft notice was received
and off to serve my country, I sped.

Thirteen months later
with Ellen just born
I left to fight a war in Vietnam
leaving you very forlorn.

While I was there
I got medals galore,
A few for just being there
others for bravery and valor.

While I came back in one piece
and for years seemed okay,
I had no idea that PTSD
was busy gnawing away.

Physically sound
but mentally wounded,
no medal for that
not even a mention.

And not just to me
Did the war take its toll,
wounds surely developed
within you as well.

Most who are wounded by combat
receive recognition of such,
The Purple Heart Medal
is the appropriate touch.

And since your wounds also come
from combat as anyone can see,
this Purple Heart Medal
is awarded to you, Judy, from me.

For all the years of putting up with me,
with all the grief, turmoil and flack,
for the love and support that you always gave
in spite of what little I gave back.

No one deserves this more.
I LOVE YOU!
Howard

1st Cavalry Div's Company E Finds Enemy In His Own Yard

BY PFC LONSWAY
Cavalair Staff Writer

LZ JANE — Winding through the thick jungle growth up and down the steep hills several miles southwest of Quang Tri lies a small trail. It crosses a stream and makes a sharp bend to the south. Lack of vegetative growth and visible footprints in the soft mud along the stream are evidence that the trail is used by someone quite frequently and recently. The moon is bright as five figures make their way along the trail. Unsuspecting, they round the bend and cross the stream. Suddenly, they are hit by a barrage of automatic weapons fire from the thick growth that borders the trail. Three of them fall to the ground dead and the two others manage to escape perhaps wounded. Silently, several figures make their way from the jungle to the bodies on the trail. They spend only a few seconds at each body and then move on. Shortly, they join the others back in the thick brush.

NVA SOLDIERS

The men that fell from the fire were NVA soldiers. The men in the brush were Skytroopers from the 1st Battalion, 5th Cavalry's new reconnaissance unit, Company "E". They had conducted a successful ambush, set up trip flares and then moved back under cover to wait again for the enemy.

The company was formed and first became operational on the 1st of June as a result of a new U.S. Army policy stating that all battalions would form a new company to be used for reconnaissance work.

"Our primary job is to conduct recon work for the battalion," explained First Lieutenant Michael Moon (Greenwood, Ind.), the commanding officer for the company. "We move into areas of suspected enemy positions," he continued "and determine the size of the element if possible. Our job in most cases is not to make initial contact but rather to recon the area."

Lieutenant Colonel Gregory Troutman, commander of the 1st Bn., 5th Cav, described the company as "the best small fighting unit in the division."

Presently composed of a large recon platoon, the unit will eventually have a radar platoon and a mortar platoon to go with the recon platoon.

During the first ten days of July, the recon Skytroopers conducted numerous ambushes that netted nine NVA killed and one POW. They also captured eight AK-47s and one SKS in the successful operations some 13 miles southeast of Quang Tri City.

BEST COMPANY

Boasting the best company in the battalion, First Sergeant Willie Hightower (Macon, Ga.) attributed the success of the unit to its "good leaders and men" and "its training program. We had the opportunity to get together for several hours of instruction before going out," he explained. "Occasionally," he continued "we meet to discuss a recent operation to try and learn from our mistakes."

At various times the unit functions as a ready reaction force, moving in to support any unit in trouble. On July 7, Company "B" came under heavy fire 12 miles southeast of Quang Tri City. Two squads of Echo's recon platoon were in the vicinity providing security for engineers blowing bunkers, discovered earlier by Bravo Company. The recon Cavalrymen gave fire post to Bravo and helped to carry out the wounded.

1LT Moon cited another instance where a Chinook helicopter carrying the mail was fired upon by a sniper just outside LZ Jane. In less than 15 minutes the recon platoon was on their way out to the area where the fire was believed to have come. They received fire shortly after approaching the suspected position and returned a heavy volume of fire until they silenced the hidden riflemen.

Patience, in the form of not moving for hours at a time and not making any sound is absolutely necessary in reconnaissance work. Specialist 4 Casey Jones (Erie, Colo.), a dog handler with the 25th Scout Dog Platoon at LZ Jane recently accompanied two squads of the recon platoon on a day ambush 13 miles southeast of Quang Tri City. "They were one of the best ambush teams I've been out with, especially for noise discipline," he remarked.

1st Cavalry Division Combat Manpower Chart

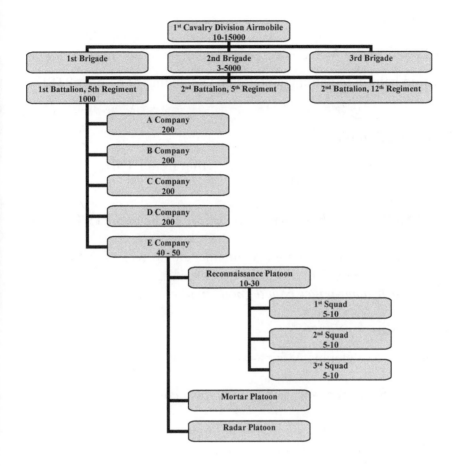

The numbers for the elements of the 2nd Brigade are estimates of the combat infantry manpower, but only during my tour in Vietnam. They do not include support personnel, which can be as high as ten men for every one combat soldier.

Resources

In addition to the Vet Centers, here are some other resources you may find helpful in gaining a better understanding of combat PTSD.

Books and Pamphlets

Veterans and Families' Guide to Recovering from PTSD – *www.Amazon.com*

Tears of a Warrior – *http://www.mophsf.org/* (Click on PTS BOOK)

Readjustment Problems among Vietnam Veterans: The Etiology of Combat-related Post-Traumatic Stress Disorders – *http://www.trauma-pages.com/a/goodwin.php*

Internet Sites

Department of Veterans Affairs - *www.va.gov*

Combat PTSD Forum - *www.mycombatptsd.com*

Military.com – PTSD - *http://www.military.com/benefits/veterans-health-care/posttraumatic-stress-disorder-overview.html*

Coping with PTSD - *http://www.familyofavet.com/coping_with_PTSD.html*

National Center for PTSD - *http://www.ptsd.va.gov/public/index.asp*

Family of a Vet - *http://familyofavet.com*

Vet Center Home Page - *http://www.vetcenter.va.gov*

Many of the above internet sites have links to other web sites that may provide additional useful information.

Glossary

AGENT ORANGE - An herbicide used to defoliate forest areas that might conceal NVA and VC forces and to destroy crops that might feed the enemy

AIR MEDAL - Awarded for 25 Combat Air Assaults

AIT - Advanced Individual Training

AO - Area of Operation

ARVN - Army of the Republic of Vietnam

AWOL - Absent Without Leave

BOONIES - Rural and jungle areas of Vietnam where most of the fighting occurred

C & P - Compensation and Pension

CHARLIE - Commonly used as a substitute name for VC or NVA

CIB - Combat Infantry Badge

CO - Conscientious Objector

COBRA - Bell AH-1 Helicopter - also called a Cobra Gunship

DAV - Disabled American Veteran

DI - Drill Instructor

DMZ - Demilitarized Zone

EMDR - Eye Movement Desensitization Reprocessing

FB - Fire Base

FNG - Fuckin' New Guy

GI - Government Issue - slang for American soldier

GRUNT - General term for an infantryman

HUEY - Bell UH-1 Helicopter - also called a Slick

KIA - Killed in Action

KLICK - One Kilometer - approximately 6/10 of a mile

KP - Kitchen Patrol

LOACH - Hughes OH-6 Cayuse Helicopter - LOH (Light Observation Helicopter)

LP - Listening Post

LRRP - Long Range Recon Patrol – pronounced "lerp"

LRRP RATIONS - Dehydrated Meals

LZ - Landing Zone

MEDCAP - Medical Civil Action Programs

MEDEVAC - Medical Evacuation Helicopter

MIA - Missing in Action

MP - Military Police

NAPALM - Extremely flammable, gasoline-based fire bomb that can cover an area 270 feet long by 75 feet wide when dropped from the air in large drums

NCO - Non Commissioned Officer - Sergeant

NVA - North Vietnamese Army

OCS - Officer Candidate School

P38 - Mini Can Opener

POW - Prisoner of War

PSYOPS - Psychological Operations

PT - Physical Training

PTSD - Post Traumatic Stress Disorder

PX - Post Exchange

REMF - Rear Echelon Mother Fucker

RTO - Radio Telephone Operator

SAPPER - VC or NVA soldier carrying satchel charges

SHORT-TIMER - A soldier approaching the end of his tour of duty

T & P - Total and Permanent

TOC - Tactical Operations Center

VA - Department of Veterans Affairs

VC -Viet Cong

VICTOR CHARLIE - Phonetic Alphabet for VC

VET CENTER - Community based facilities established in 1979 as part of the VA system to help veterans make successful transitions from military to civilian life

VFW - Veterans of Foreign Wars

VSO - Veteran Service Officer

WIA - Wounded in Action

Your comments are always welcome.

****

To contact me please send an email to:

hbpatrick43@gmail.com